CAMBRIDGE LIBRARY COLLECTION

Books of enduring scholarly value

Travel and Exploration

The history of travel writing dates back to the Bible, Caesar, the Vikings and the Crusaders, and its many themes include war, trade, science and recreation. Explorers from Columbus to Cook charted lands not previously visited by Western travellers, and were followed by merchants, missionaries, and colonists, who wrote accounts of their experiences. The development of steam power in the nineteenth century provided opportunities for increasing numbers of 'ordinary' people to travel further, more economically, and more safely, and resulted in great enthusiasm for travel writing among the reading public. Works included in this series range from first-hand descriptions of previously unrecorded places, to literary accounts of the strange habits of foreigners, to examples of the burgeoning numbers of guidebooks produced to satisfy the needs of a new kind of traveller - the tourist.

The Cruise of H.M.S. *Calliope* in China, Australian and East African Waters, 1887–1890

Arthur Cornwallis Evans (1860–1935) was chaplain on the steamship H.M.S. *Calliope* on a three-year voyage to Asia and Australia (January 1887 to April 1890) that covered 76,814 nautical miles (88,395 miles), with more than 500 days spent at sea. He compiled this lively account of the voyage at the request of his shipmates, drawing information from several of their journals, and published it in Portsmouth in 1890 before the crew dispersed. It contains both brief factual entries about the progress of the voyage and more sustained descriptions of life on board ship and in port, including some naval culinary 'delicacies', an encounter with a robber in Hong Kong, the Russian fortifications at Vladivostok, fireworks in Sydney celebrating the centenary of New South Wales, the opening of Calliope Dock in Auckland (still in use today), visits to several Pacific islands, cricket matches and regattas, and an eclipse of the sun.

T0364316

Cambridge University Press has long been a pioneer in the reissuing of out-of-print titles from its own backlist, producing digital reprints of books that are still sought after by scholars and students but could not be reprinted economically using traditional technology. The Cambridge Library Collection extends this activity to a wider range of books which are still of importance to researchers and professionals, either for the source material they contain, or as landmarks in the history of their academic discipline.

Drawing from the world-renowned collections in the Cambridge University Library and other partner libraries, and guided by the advice of experts in each subject area, Cambridge University Press is using state-of-the-art scanning machines in its own Printing House to capture the content of each book selected for inclusion. The files are processed to give a consistently clear, crisp image, and the books finished to the high quality standard for which the Press is recognised around the world. The latest print-on-demand technology ensures that the books will remain available indefinitely, and that orders for single or multiple copies can quickly be supplied.

The Cambridge Library Collection brings back to life books of enduring scholarly value (including out-of-copyright works originally issued by other publishers) across a wide range of disciplines in the humanities and social sciences and in science and technology.

The Cruise
of H.M.S. *Calliope*
in China, Australian
and East African Waters
1887–1890

ARTHUR CORNWALLIS EVANS

CAMBRIDGE
UNIVERSITY PRESS

CAMBRIDGE UNIVERSITY PRESS

Cambridge, New York, Melbourne, Madrid, Cape Town,
Singapore, São Paolo, Delhi, Mexico City

Published in the United States of America by Cambridge University Press, New York

www.cambridge.org
Information on this title: www.cambridge.org/9781108045889

© in this compilation Cambridge University Press 2012

This edition first published 1890
This digitally printed version 2012

ISBN 978-1-108-04588-9 Paperback

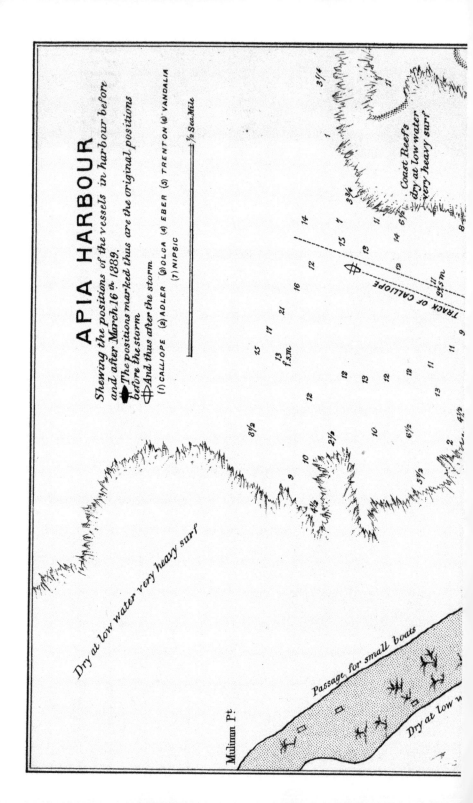

APIA HARBOUR

Shewing the positions of the vessels in harbour before and after March 16th 1889.

The positions marked thus ↑ are the original positions before the storm

⊕ And thus after the storm

(1) CALLIOPE (2) ADLER (3) OLGA (4) EBER (5) TRENTON (6) VANDALIA (7) NIPSIC

← ½ Sea Mile →

Dry at low water very heavy surf

Coast Reefs dry at low water very heavy surf

TRACK OF CALLIOPE

Mulinuu Pt.

Passage for small boats

Dry at low water

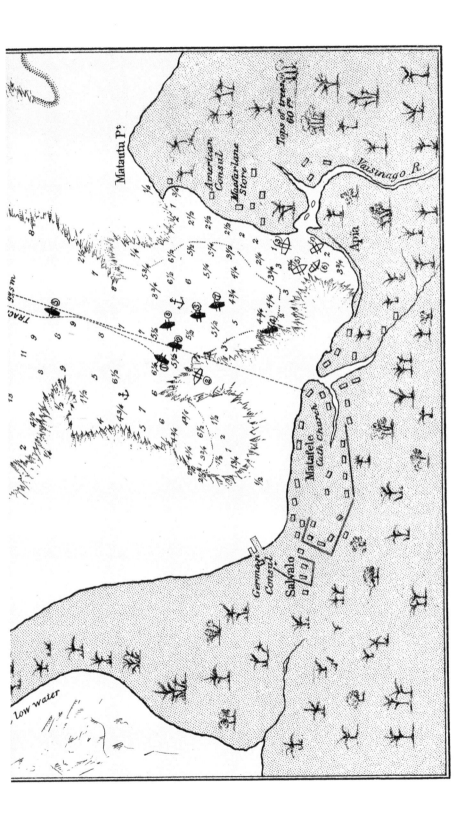

THE

CRUISE OF H.M.S. "CALLIOPE"

IN

CHINA,

AUSTRALIAN AND EAST AFRICAN WATERS.

1887—1890.

BY THE

REV. A. C. EVANS, M.A.,

CHAPLAIN R.N.

1890.

GRIFFIN AND CO.,

Publishers to Her Majesty.

2, THE HARD, PORTSMOUTH.

RICHARD CLAY AND SONS, LIMITED,
LONDON AND BUNGAY.

PREFACE.

THE following pages have been thrown together very hurriedly, during the last few weeks, in response to a wish expressed by several of the ship's company that there should be some such record of the Commission. They are not meant to give by any means a complete account of the cruise, but rather a record of the most important events, with a few notes about some of the places visited. My thanks are due to all those who have kindly placed their journals at my disposal, and to Mr. H. W. Richmond, midshipman, R.N., for the plan of Apia Harbour.

It has been necessary, not only to write hastily, but also to print hastily, in order to have the journal ready for distribution before the pennant is hauled down and the crew scattered to the four corners of England. In consequence of the want of due revision it is almost certain that many mistakes will have crept in here and there; but in spite of all blemishes I hope that the " Cruise of H.M.S. *Calliope* " may be a useful memento of an eventful and interesting Commission.

A. C. E.

H.M.S. *Calliope,*
April, 1890.

THE

CRUISE OF H.M.S. "CALLIOPE."

1887.

COMMISSIONING AT PORTSMOUTH AND VOYAGE TO CHINA VIA THE CAPE.

January 25th.—Captain H. C. Kane commissioned H.M.S. *Calliope* at Portsmouth for service on the China station. This was ordered to be done with all possible despatch, and a working party of 120 men was sent to assist in drawing stores. The ship commissioned in dry dock, the feathering arrangements of the screw having broken down on trial. The first afternoon was used for drawing sails, getting them ready for bending, and getting on board and stowing provisions. Dockyard people worked night and day about the screw. As the ship could easily be got ready in other respects before the screw was completed, leave was given each night while in dock, and with the satisfactory result that no one broke it.

26th.—Completed the drawing and stowing of stores and bent sails.

27th.—Screw completed at 10 A.M. Floated out of dry dock, proceeded to Spithead and swung for adjustment of compasses. Powder lighters came alongside; took in powder and shell. Midnight, ready for sea.

28th.—Admiral Sir George O. Willes, K.C.B., came on board and inspected the ship at general and fire quarters, &c.

29th.—Dense fog, which lifted a little at 11 A.M. Weighed and proceeded towards St. Helen's, but fog coming down again, anchored off that place. Issued arms and accoutrements.

30th.—Dense fog, which lifted about 1 P.M. Started on a week's commissioning cruise.

31st.—Cruising in the Channel, stationing the ship's company, exercising them at quarters night and day, fire stations, making sail, shortening sail, working ship under sail, &c. Sighted H.M.S. *Cordelia*, which had also commissioned on January 25th, and put to sea shortly before the *Calliope*.

February 2nd.—Began steam trial at 10 A.M., but barometer falling rapidly and sea getting up, discontinued it after two hours: the speed attained was fourteen knots. Anchored at 10 P.M. in Portland Roads. Weather outside very thick and blowing hard.

5th.—Weather moderating, proceeded to sea. Made sail and exercised tacking, wearing, &c. Bore up for St. Catherine's (*6th*), and reached Spithead the following morning.

7th.—Proceeded up harbour, and remained till February 24th. The dockyard during that time made good defects. Drew stores to complete for the China station—viz., extra sails, ropes, &c.

20th.—H.M.S. *Cordelia* sailed for China.

22nd.—Her Majesty the Queen arrived at Portsmouth in H.M. yacht *Alberta*, on her way to Windsor, and landed at Clarence Yard. Dressed ship with masthead flags, manned yards, full guard of marines. The Commander-in-Chief inspected the ship, *i.e.*, mustered the ship's company and walked round the ship.

23rd. — Commander-in-Chief inspected ship with regard to gunnery arrangements.

24th.—Proceeded out of harbour and worked up for full-speed trials by the Steam Reserve. After half an hour at full speed, obliged to stop and repack gland of piston-rod. Ran a three hours' trial, two hours with natural draught, and one hour with forced draught, with the following results :—

$$\text{Draught} \ldots \begin{cases} \text{Forward} \ldots . 18 \text{ ft. 4 in.} \\ \text{Aft} \ldots . . . 21 \text{ ft. 3 in.} \end{cases}$$

	Natural Draught.	Forced Draught.
Steam in Boilers	84·5	85·75
Vacuum { Forward	25·25	26·0
Vacuum { Aft	23·87	24·5
Revolutions per minute.	79·85	86·48
Mean Pressure { High	35·08	43·05
Mean Pressure { Low	11·87	15·37
Indicated H.P. { High.	1412·3	1875·61
Indicated H.P. { Low	1409·53	1972·95
Total I.H.P.	2821·83	3848·56
Speed	13·67	14·52

Anchored at Spithead after trial.

25th.—Swung for adjustment of compasses, and anchored off Cowes.

26th.—Weighed at 8 A.M. and proceeded down Channel, working up for full speed trial, and worked up to 13·5, but the packing of high-pressure piston-rod

B 2

gave out, so trial ceased at 3.15 P.M. Made fast to
buoy in Plymouth Sound at 10 P.M.

27th and *28th.*—At Plymouth, getting in a capstan
engine for H.M.S. *Leander,* and having it secured by
the dockyard authorities.

March 1st.—A further steam trial being deemed un-
necessary, the time came to say " Good-bye " to England,
and at 5 P.M. the ship started on her voyage to China
viâ the Cape.

2nd to *11th.*—The weather crossing the Bay was all
that could be desired, water smooth, wind from the N.E.
After passing Cape Finisterre, encountered a considerable S.E. swell and light winds from that direction, till
lat. 41° 30′ N. was reached, when the wind backed to
N.E. and blew fresh for twenty-four hours. Then getting
into the S.W. the wind remained ahead but light, till
Madeira was reached on the morning of the 11th.
During the cruise sail was used whenever possible
without getting off the course. A considerable amount
of drill was got through, making and shortening sail,
up and down top-gallant masts, working ship, general
quarters, fire stations, &c. It appears that the ship
steams well in smooth water and with little or no wind,
but any head sea at once brings down the speed considerably. She is lively, but rolls with an easy motion.

11th.—Arrived at Funchal and went through the
customary salutes, completed with coal, &c. H.M.S. *Wye*
arrived from Bermuda during the night *en route* for
England.

13th.—Proceeded to sea in the evening ; just able to
carry fore and aft sail to a stiff breeze.

20th.—Arrived at St. Vincent, and coaled. Here a

curious hill, whose outline is supposed to resemble the profile of Washington's face, is pointed out to the visitor, and certainly forms a remarkable feature in the landscape. The *Calliope* Cricket Club here played their first match, which resulted in a victory for the St. Vincent eleven.

22nd.—Sailed at 7 A.M., and arrived on the evening of the next day at Porto Praya in St. Jago, one of the Cape de Verde islands, in time for a grand *fête* in honour of the birth of a son and heir to the Crown Prince of Portugal ;—the young Prince Luiz Filippe, born March 1st, 1887, is now himself Crown Prince in consequence of the succession of his father to the throne.

24th.—Weighed about 8 A.M., and began the long passage to the Cape, steering to cross the line in about 26° W. longitude, the trade-wind blowing with a force of three to four.

25th to *31st.*—The trade gradually got lighter till in lat. 4° N. it was altogether lost, and steam was raised about 250' from the equator. Crossed the line on March 31st, in long. 26° W. There were a goodly number on board who had never crossed the line before, and it must no doubt have been a source of satisfaction to them that Father Neptune did not make his appearance, for these visits, although much appreciated by those who have no longer to submit to the shaving-brush, are not quite so amusing to the uninitiated. The first of the S.E. trade was picked up on the afternoon of the 31st, but very light, and steam was not dispensed with till the following day.

April 1st to *30th.*—Carried the S.E. trade to about lat. 20° S., that is, till abreast the island of Trinidad.

After passing about 100′ to the westward of Trinidad very light and variable winds were encountered, chiefly from the E. and N.E., the weather remaining fine on the whole. The ship's company were exercised on most evenings, and the watch as requisite for trimming, making, shortening sail, &c., and also firing at general quarters. Thus passed the month of April without any incident of note to break the monotony of routine and sea-life. On April 30th the Cape was still 840′ distant. Although now in lat. 37° S. there was no sign of the expected favourable westerly wind.

May 5th to 16th.—Dropped anchor in Simon's Bay about 10.30 P.M. on May 5th, forty-two days out from Porto Praya. The order "let go the starboard anchor" sounded very pleasantly in everybody's ears after such a long spell of sea-time. The Cape was new ground to the majority of the ship's company, and therefore in addition to the pleasure of once more setting foot on shore, there was the interest of seeing a new place ; but a more immediate pleasure was even more welcome, viz., that of once more receiving letters and papers after so long a silence. A boat from the flag-ship, H.M.S. *Raleigh,* was soon alongside with six bags of mails, which at once gave full employment to all hands. The ships in harbour were H.M.S. *Raleigh, Flora,* and *Wrangler.*

The days spent in Simon's Bay were fully occupied with coaling, refitting, and victualling ship, and in giving leave. General leave was given to the starboard watch on May 9th, and to the port watch on May 10th, and was no doubt as much appreciated as it was deserved. On May 15th Admiral Sir W. Hunt-Grubbe, Commander-in-Chief at the Cape, visited the ship.

16th.—On Monday, May 16th, the anchor was weighed at 8.30 A.M., and the long sailing passage to New Anjer began. The track chosen took the ship well to the southward, but although lat. 42° 50′ S. was reached no strong steady winds were experienced, and in consequence the passage proved a long one. Throughout the passage drills and routine were carried out.

28th.—In lat. 42° 48′ S., and long. 52° E., the thermometer suddenly fell 10° F., and shortly afterwards a large iceberg was observed on the port bow, but at a considerable distance. All through the westerly winds, and to near lat. 30° S., the ship was followed by vast quantities of albatross, Cape pigeon, &c., but by far the most interesting event during this trip was the sight of a rather rare and very curious phenomenon known as a " milky sea." On June 21st at dusk, the ship was found to be sailing in very phosphorescent water which, as darkness closed in, became quite white, and when contrasted with the overhanging clouds presented a very weird and ghostly appearance. It seemed as if the water had by some magic been changed into a vast plain of freshly-fallen snow, stretching as far as the eye could reach. This appearance lasted throughout the night; by day nothing unusual was observed in the condition of the water.

This phenomenon is no doubt due to the presence in the water of myriads of luminous " infusoria." The ship at the time was in lat. 16° S., long. 107° E. A " milky sea " has frequently been observed in the Indian Ocean by ships making passages from Aden to Bombay, or *vice versâ*.

On long sea trips like the present the canteen is a

great boon to the ship's company, as it enables them to enjoy rather more varied fare than when they are reduced to "pure navy." What devices are resorted to when the resources of the canteen are exhausted may be gathered from the following extracts from a blue-jacket's journal:—

"*Receipt for Navy Plum Duff.*—Procure about twelve pounds of flour, according to the number of men to be fed, each man allowed one pound, and about two pounds of raisins. Stand about four yards from the kettle in which you are going to mix your duff, and pitch them into it ; all that goes outside you eat. Add one pound of salt suet cut up into lumps, some salt, and half a gallon of water : mix up together. Then procure a canvas bag to boil it in—I have seen towels utilized for this purpose. When it is cut it looks just like a huge india-rubber ball with brown spots few and far between. It is as heavy as lead. I pity any one who may fall overboard after a good feed of this delicacy.

"*Mang.*—This is a very unintelligible name, and I am sorry to say that none of these dishes will be found in any book of cookery. Mang, however, is made by a very simple process, viz.: Procure a quantity of biscuit, pound it into a powder, and it is ready for use. This is gene-rally mixed with pea-soup. The next triumph of the culinary art is *Hum Durgan—alias* hummy dum. It is made as follows :—Procure some small pieces of bis-cuit, place them in a frying-pan with some fat, and when the biscuit has become soft, add salt and pepper. This is very nice.

"The next is *Pow Sow.* Of course it will be seen that this biscuit being hard is also brittle, therefore there is a great deal of dust. This dust can be returned to the ship's steward, and you can have whole biscuit in lieu of it, or else, as is generally the case, it is utilized to make pow sow. You place the dust and small biscuit in a kettle, leave it to soak till quite soft, then mix it with flour, raisins, and sugar. Bake it in a dish. This is found to be very acceptable for tea."

June 25th.—About 2.30 P.M. Christmas Island was sighted on the port bow. This island, situated about 220 miles south of Java Head, is about nine miles in length and nearly square : it is covered with trees, principally limes and cocoa-nuts, the tops of which may be seen from a distance of thirty miles in clear weather.

27th.—At daylight the entrance to Sunda Strait was sighted, and the same evening the ship anchored off New Anjer, forty-two days out from the Cape.

Sunda Strait, through which passes a large part of the trade of Singapore, Batavia, and other ports in the China and Java seas, separates the large islands of Java and Sumatra. There are several islands in the Strait, but the most conspicuous and most interesting of these is Krakatoa. The following short account of this volcano and its eruptions is taken from the *China Sea Directory* :—

" The volcano of Krakatoa Island was in eruption in the year 1680, and although included within the category of active volcanoes, it remained in a state of comparative inactivity for upwards of 200 years.

" In the year 1883, on May 20th, the volcano burst into eruption, accompanied by earthquakes, which were severely felt at Batavia, and at the same time vast showers of pumice and ashes were projected to a great

distance.   This eruption was observed from the Imperial
German ship *Elizabeth*, and on the following day, when
100 miles from Krakatoa, a shower of dust was experienced which was estimated to become a layer one inch
in thickness in twenty-four hours, and dust was observed
to be still falling when the vessel had gained a position
300 miles south-west of Sunda Strait.   On 26th August,
1883, Krakatoa again burst into eruption, and of such a
terrible nature that miles of coast on both sides of the
strait were wholly devastated, and multitudes of people
perished.   On the 27th August a succession of earthquake waves swept the shores of the strait, utterly
destroying the towns of Anjer, Merak, Tyringin, and
Telok Betung, together with some of the lighthouses
on both shores.   This remarkable disturbance of the
sea made itself felt in various parts of the world upon
the same date, notably in Australia and Southern Africa,
also at Karachi in India.   The vast amount of pumice
which lay upon the surface of the sea, in some places
many feet in thickness, gave an appearance as if the
ocean bed had appeared above water."

New Anjer is the name of the town built to replace
Anjer, which was destroyed in 1883.

June 28*th.*—Weighed at 6 A.M., and proceeded for
Singapore through Banka Strait.   Arrived at Singapore
about 2 P.M. on July 2nd, and communicated with
H.M.S. *Orion.*   Here everybody expected to get a few
days in harbour after so much sea-work ; but this expectation was not to be fulfilled, for the very unwelcome
orders were received to coal at once and proceed to
Hong-Kong at ten knots.   The ship at once went
alongside the Tanjong Pagar wharf, and coaling began,

and was carried on vigorously far into the night. Under these circumstances very little could be seen of the town and neighbourhood.

THE CHINA STATION.

At daylight on July 3rd sailed for Hong-Kong. The passage was a quick and pleasant one, and occupied only six days. Anchor was dropped in Hong-Kong harbour about 10 A.M. on July 9th. The entrance to Hong-Kong harbour is very beautiful, and the harbour itself is one of the finest and most picturesque in the world. The lofty hills on the mainland look soft and mysterious with their alternations of light and shade, but are very bare of trees. The island of Hong-Kong lies off the mouth of the Canton river; it is separated from the mainland by the fine harbour and the narrow passes which afford entrance to it at each end. The British colony consists of the island of Hong-Kong and the peninsula of Kowloon, where there is a good dock. Hong-Kong was ceded to England in 1841, and Kowloon in 1860. The island is about eleven miles long, and varies from two to five miles in breadth; it is very hilly, the highest point—Victoria Peak—being over 1,800 feet. The hills have been well planted with trees, which have much improved the climate as well as the appearance of the island. The principal town— Victoria—faces the harbour, and lies between the water's edge and the high hills which rise almost immediately behind it. It is a large and important place of over 130,000 inhabitants, a large proportion of whom are Chinese. The town contains some good streets and many fine buildings; and both the town and its surroundings, it is said, have been much improved of late years.

A very fine aqueduct recently completed forms an excellent roadway as well as a waterway. As it winds round the hills a succession of beautiful views of the harbour are obtained, which it would be difficult to surpass.   Other objects of interest are the beautiful and carefully-kept Gardens, the Cathedral, the Naval Hospital, the Happy Valley, a cemetery where for once nature and art have combined to banish all that is ugly and depressing, and to introduce everything beautiful and consoling.   The Happy Valley has a strange neighbour ; only separated from it by the main road is the racecourse.   A tramway, since completed, was in course of construction for conveying passengers and goods from the town as far as the Gap, that is, the greater part of the way to the Peak, where most of the Europeans have houses.   The journey up to the present has usually been made in a chair carried by four Chinamen, as the hill is far too steep to admit of the "jinricksha."   But although shut out from the Peak, the jinrickshas have their own way in the town, and afford a most convenient and very cheap mode of conveyance.

Hong-Kong is the great meeting place for the trade of the East; in 1888 shipping to the extent of nearly six and a half million tons entered the port.   This of course means that a very large number of seamen of all nations are constantly passing through, and provide abundant work for the chaplain of the Seamen's Mission, whose pretty church is situated at West Point, close to the Sailors' Home.

The few days spent at Hong-Kong were fully occupied with coaling, refitting and provisioning ship, preparatory to the cruise to meet the Admiral in Japanese waters. General leave was given to both watches; a day and a half on shore among the strange sights and sounds of Hong-Kong was a delightful change after so much cruising. Some of the impressions produced may be gathered from the following extract taken from the journal referred to above :—

HONG-KONG BY NIGHT.

" Hong-Kong by night presents a vastly different appearance to the same town by day. Nearly all the shops are lit up by gas, whilst coloured lanterns of all kinds hang outside, giving the street quite a festive look. The shops are well stocked, the gilt labels marked with Chinese characters, which show, I suppose, the worth of the goods, glitter and shine on the shelves and give the place quite a gay look. Here and there a long-tailed celestial flits noiselessly about the shop seeming very busy; but in reality he is doing nothing. In one corner may be seen, squatted on his haunches, the shrivelled proprietor, his small eyes fixed on the entrance, waiting for customers, who are very scarce at some establishments—there he sits, for hours never moving or speaking. At street corners stand the water-melon and ice-cream stalls, their owners yelling out some sort of jargon continuously. Numerous customers, young and old, flock round these stalls, eating their cent slices of melon or sipping their ice with great care as if they were afraid of being frozen. I have often

wished that I could sketch, so that I might have had
portraits of a few of that crowd. Further on you come
to an eating-house, but you are able to smell these
places afar off. Here they are; the windows are open.
You don't see the juicy sirloin, or the savoury beef pie
steaming away; bless you, no! Instead, you have five
or six rows of roast fowls on hooks, hung up to dry. The
bodies of these fowls look as if they had been French
polished. Inside the window there is a large copper
full of soup, boiling away right merrily; now and again
you can see pieces of vegetable rise to the surface
followed by something else. The half-naked and greasy-
looking cooks fly round this copper like flies in a strange
house, each one throwing the remains of a well-picked
fowl into this combination of mysteries, or else he drops
a piece of—well, I don't know what it is! At any
rate, they do a good trade, so I suppose it must be
good. I should have to be very drunk before I dined
there; but the Chinese are not particular as a rule what
they eat; they don't mind as long as it fills up and is
cheap, and they think you are the same. We are now in
the back slums, few and far between are the gas lamps,
throwing a faint light around. All at once you are
startled by the figure of a loosely-clad silent individual
flitting by you like a ghost; suddenly he stops, takes a
mat from under his arm, lays it out on the pathway,
then down he goes on top of it, and goes to sleep. He
lives there, you know. They lie scattered about in all
directions. I was quietly walking along one of these
streets one night, when all at once over I went. 'I beg
your pardon,' says I, to a miserably clad object which
rose up as if out of the ground. He looked very weird

and ghostly. I had serious thoughts of taking to my heels, but he suddenly vanished. I felt a tap on the shoulder, and turned round to confront the tall straight figure of one of the Sikh police, who inquired if there was anything wrong. I told him about it ; he laughed, and quietly told me that the wretch would have stabbed me if he had not appeared at that moment. The great respect the Chinese have for these tall, fierce-looking Sikhs is quite remarkable. I never saw in all my life such obedience paid to the police ; their word is law ; they scatter a crowd like chaff before the wind. They are the right men in the right place."

July 17th.—Hong-Kong in July is unpleasantly warm, in consequence the prospect of getting into a cooler climate was welcome. A start was made on Sunday, July 17th, when about 7 A.M. the *Calliope* slipped her buoy and proceeded under steam through the Lymoon Pass, to join the Admiral in Japanese waters.

A fairly quick passage was made to Nagasaki, which was reached about sunset on July 21st. The entrance to the beautiful harbour was most striking ; although on a much smaller scale than Hong-Kong, the harbour is even more beautiful ; it is approached through a narrow channel winding between hills covered with verdure. Just off the entrance is the island of Pappenburg, memorable as the spot where, some 300 years ago, native Christians were thrown down from the precipitous cliffs on the rocks below. Nagasaki has now a population of about 40,000 ; it is remarkable as having been the only Japanese trading port open to foreigners between the years 1623 and 1857. Formerly it had a large trade, but though much of this has now been turned aside to Yokohama and other ports, yet it is still a place of importance on account of the large supplies of good coal obtained from Takosima.

On anchoring, saluted the Japanese flag with twenty-one guns, and the American Admiral, who happened to be in port with two ships, with thirteen guns. The reports were echoed and re-echoed from the hills on either side of the narrow harbour, till the whole country seemed saluting.

The narrow streets and quaint Japanese houses, the shops with curious tortoiseshell, metal, and porcelain work, the quaint dresses and charming manners of the people, all combine to interest and amuse. A very fine view of the town and harbour is to be obtained from the Sinto Temple, which is approached by a long flight of steps.

A Church of England Mission is at work in Nagasaki, and a well-ordered Sailors' Home supplies needful accommodation for seamen.

July 22nd.—The following day was fully occupied with coaling, and at daylight on the 23rd the anchor was weighed, and a start made for Hako-date.

July 27th.—Arrived at Hako-date about 9 A.M. on the 27th, after a very calm passage ; expected to find the Admiral here with the fleet, but he was absent on a short cruise. Hako-date is one of the most important towns in Yezo, the northern island of Japan. It has neither the beauty nor the interest of Nagasaki or Yokohama, but to make up for that it is more out of the track of Europeans. There is a good harbour. The town consists chiefly of long straggling streets, full of small shops. Immediately behind the town is a high wooded hill which affords a good walk, and a fine view at the top as a reward. Close to the town are some pretty gardens and tea-houses, and not far from these is a museum very neatly kept, though not, as yet, very well stocked. The orderly conduct, good humour, and politeness of the people are very noticeable ; also the care bestowed on the children, who always seem to have a good time.

On July 30th Admiral Sir R. Vesey Hamilton, K.C.B., arrived with nine ships of the China Squadron, viz., *Audacious* (flag-ship), *Leander*, *Constance*, *Heroine*, *Swift*, *Linnet*, *Merlin*, *Wanderer*, and *Alacrity*. Later in the day the *Cordelia* and *Satellite* also arrived. The former ship was eagerly looked out for by many on board, and at once set down as " chummy ship."

The China Squadron are now in the midst of the usual summer cruise in Japanese waters; they have already visited the inland sea, and Yokohama ; we have therefore lost the opportunity of seeing much that is most interesting. It would have been worth while to have seen the capital of a country which is said to possess a written history extending over 2,500 years, and whose Emperor, the 121st of his race, belongs to a dynasty which stretches down in an unbroken line from the year 660 B.C.

August 1*st.*—Weighed, and proceeded outside for prize-firing, which was cut short by bad weather; returned on the morning of the 3rd in time to sail with the fleet at 5 P.M. The *Leander* remained behind to wait for mails.

With so many ships together there is much rivalry at

sail drill and other evolutions, in most of which the *Calliope* holds her own very well.

August 4th to *9th.*—After a pleasant cruise northwards along the coast of Yezo, arrived at Otenanai shortly after midnight, and anchored between one and two miles from the shore. This is a large bay, and affords good anchorage. Its shores are dotted with numerous villages and hamlets, one of which gives its name to the bay ; another and more important is named Otara. A good deal of amusement, and some good curios are to be obtained by a leisurely look through the little village shops, whose owners are very polite, and very ready to make a good bargain for themselves.

About twenty-five miles from Otara, and accessible by a small railway which skirts the edge of the bay for some miles before it turns inland, is Saporo, the capital of Yezo. The journey occupies rather less than two hours. Saporo lies on a broad plain with fine wooded hills rising at a few miles' distance; a river runs near the town, and is spanned by a fine railway bridge; it is said to afford some excellent fishing. The streets are broad and straight, but the houses for the most part are small and mean-looking. There are many signs of Western civilization in Saporo ; amongst these may be reckoned an excellent hotel, an agricultural college, a brewery, managed on the most approved German principles, a sauce manufactory, a flour mill, &c.

August 9th.—The *Leander* arrived with mails on the morning of the 8th, and on the following day, at 6 P.M., the fleet sailed for the coast of Russian Tartary. The *Leander* again remained behind ; this time to await the arrival of the *Sapphire.* These two ships joined the fleet on August 11th. On the passage across a good deal of fog was encountered, and in consequence night and day were made hideous by the steam sirens of a dozen vessels. On the evening of August 12th the fleet came to an anchor in Amur Bay during a thick fog. When the fog lifted, the fleet weighed and proceeded to within about four miles of the entrance to the harbour of Vladivostock; where anchors were again let go, and the *Linnet* only went into the harbour in order to obtain permission for ships to enter. Vladivostock is the head-quarters of the Russian Navy in these waters; it has a floating dock, and is an excellent harbour in summer time, but in winter is ice-bound; in consequence, the Russians are said to be very anxious to obtain possession of one of the fine Corean harbours which are open throughout the year.

Formerly the Russians allowed any number of foreign war-ships to enter their harbours, but now they have limited the number to two of any one nation at a time.

On this occasion the *Calliope* and the *Linnet* were ordered to enter the harbour, the object being to obtain fresh provisions for the fleet. The entrance is narrow and winding, and very strongly fortified; the harbour affords first-rate shelter, as, once inside, the sea is completely lost sight of.

Anchored about 2 P.M. on August 14th; the usual salutes were exchanged. A considerable Russian squadron was in port at the time, two ironclads, one of them the *Dimitri Domskoi*, and three corvettes, of which the finest was the *Rynda*, a smart-looking craft, and as she is a "ship of the guard," carries a picked crew; at the present time she is on a trip round the world, having on board the Grand Duke Michaelovitch, and is bound next for Japan and Australia. During our stay, the Russians were busily occupied with "landing-parties," "torpedo attacks at night," &c. Vladivostock is now a considerable place, and seems likely to develop into a large town.

There are some fine business buildings and Government buildings. The largest stores seem to be in the hands of Germans. Most of the ordinary houses have stone foundations raised three or four feet above the ground, and the rest of the structure of wood. The footpaths at the side of the street are also formed of wooden boards, in some places much the worse for wear. The Naval Club kindly invited the officers to become honorary members during the *Calliope's* stay in port.

On the 19th a bazaar and *fête* was held in the Governor's grounds in aid of an orphan asylum. In many respects this resembled a similar affair in England; there were stalls of all kinds of useless articles, bands playing, little girls carrying round small nosegays which they sold at exorbitant prices; but in two ways there was a noticeable difference: first, although the goods were displayed in a number of different stalls, yet you were not allowed to buy anything that might strike your fancy; all you could do was to buy one or more tickets for a sort of large general raffle, into which everything was put, and take your chance of what fell to your lot. The second point of difference was in the refreshment stall, the only stall where the charitably-disposed buyer was permitted to follow his inclinations; here instead of the cakes and sandwiches and ices of an English bazaar, were cheese, cold fish, caviare, and vodki.

There was some good fishing and shooting to be had in the neighbourhood. Those who indulged in sporting expeditions reported that they came from time to time on camps of Russian soldiers ; these, with the regiments in barracks at Vladivostock, make up a very considerable force in the neighbourhood.

August 19*th.*—On August 19th took in bullocks and vegetables for the fleet. The upper deck, for the time, became quite a farmyard, as bullocks were tethered between the guns, and fodder and vegetables stowed in all possible places. Sailed at noon to join the fleet at Wrangel Bay. About three hours after starting we observed an eclipse of the sun. We were at the time only about 100 miles north of the line of central eclipse, and as the weather was clear, had a good view of a most interesting phenomenon. The sun was almost entirely obscured, only a small segment near the upper limb remaining visible. A strange, unnatural twilight, suddenly took the place of bright sunshine, much to the perplexity of numerous sea birds, who began flying round the ship in a bewildered manner. This eclipse was visible as a total eclipse in Russia, Northern Asia, and Japan ; but although extensive preparations had been made to observe it, the bad weather which prevailed at most of the stations chosen prevented any but the most meagre results from being obtained, and little or nothing was added to what was previously known about the sun.

Joined the fleet outside Wrangel Bay about 5 P.M., and proceeded to St. Vladimir Bay, where we arrived about 6 P.M. on August 20th. The following afternoon was occupied with discharging bullocks to the other ships.

On the 22nd went alongside flag-ship and transferred patent fuel to her.   This was easily done, as our scuttles were almost level with her main deck, and the fuel was passed through instead of being hoisted out.

On the 24th there was a large landing-party of seamen and marines from the fleet, and a sham fight.

This is a beautiful place ; the bay is surrounded by high hills covered with thick bush and trees.   There were no signs of human habitations except the huts of a few Russian convicts.

On the 27th the fleet went outside for target-practice, and afterwards proceeded to Goshkevitch Bay, where we arrived about noon on the 29th.   This was previously an unsurveyed harbour, but the Commander-in-Chief formed the fleet in columns line abreast with light draught ships leading, and steamboats with leads going ahead of them, and in this fashion the fleet entered the bay and took up an anchorage, which proved a remarkably good one : afterwards a survey of the place was started by the navigators, and in future the entry will be made without difficulty.   This place has few attractions except for sportsmen ; the country is rough-looking and desolate, but game abounds.

September 1st.—Left Goshkevitch Bay and proceeded to the southward ; on the night of the 2nd the extreme edge of a typhoon was encountered, and the fleet " lay-to " under sail off Port Lazaref, and entered harbour the following morning.   Port Lazaref is a beautiful land-locked harbour on the northern side of a large bay ; on the southern side of the same bay there is also good anchorage, off the town of Gensan, one of the ports open to foreign commerce.   The time spent in this port

was fully occupied with work. The ship was cleared
for action, every available thing was stowed away, and
those for which room could not be found were marked
" to be thrown overboard ;" running rigging was unrove
and formed into network round the masts, mantlets
were provided between the guns and coal armour round
the conning tower, &c. Extempore torpedo defence
was placed round the ship, consisting of spars, and two
hawsers, viz., hemp hawser outside and wire further in.
These defences were inspected by the Commander-in-
Chief, and then the flag-ship's spar-torpedo launch
attempted to get in, but failed.

During our stay at Port Lazaref we were visited by
several Coreans, and among others by a chief who
afforded great amusement by the discipline he main-
tained among his followers, one of whom he summarily
turned out of the ship for speaking too familiarly to
the marine officer. The chief was evidently trying to
find out why we had come, and quite failed to under-
stand that we did not intend to annex the country.
Pleasant walks and good shooting were to be had on
shore ; a considerable amount of cultivation was seen,
rice, millet, and barley seemed to be the chief products.
The specimens of Coreans to be met with in the neighbourhood of Port Lazaref were dirty and quarrelsome
in the extreme ; they seem to have no idea of beauty
or cleanliness ; their huts are wretched structures,
disgustingly dirty, and often closely crowded together
in the villages.

A very pretty view of the little town of Lazaref was
obtained from the lofty hills which overlook the
harbour ; the houses were built on a large number of

small flat islands, separated from one another by narrow channels, and at a distance looked very pretty, but a closer view would probably have destroyed the illusion.

The area of Corea is stated to be about 85,000 square miles, and its population rather more than 10,000,000. The capital is Sëoul, near the western coast of the peninsula, a town of over 200,000 inhabitants. Of smaller towns, Gensan and Fusan, which we visited, are the most important. The religions of the people are Buddhism and Confucianism.

Naval people have now at any rate one reason to feel an interest in the future of Corea, since Bishop Corfe, for many years a naval chaplain, has undertaken the difficult but glorious task of teaching the inhabitants Christianity and cleanliness. From all appearances his work will be a difficult one, and full employment will no doubt be found for the medical staff with which he proposes to start work ; but many a hearty " God speed " will follow him, both from old friends in the service, and also from many others who, although they have no personal acquaintance with the Bishop, yet feel a deep interest in his work.

On the 9th the flag-ship and the *Calliope* proceeded into the bay to run Whiteheads, and afterwards anchored off Gensan. Communication was kept up with the fleet at night by flashing with the electric light.

Left on the 12th for the southward and arrived at Fusan on the 14th. The fleet entered the harbour in single column at about ten knots, and anchored in succession.

We here received a great surprise. A semaphore was made from the flag-ship to the effect that the

Calliope was ordered to Sydney, N.S.W., for temporary service on the Australian station. This news was received with rather mixed feelings. Australia had the name of being a first-rate station, but on the other hand we were just beginning to settle down on the China station, and to make friends in the other ships. On the following day the Commander-in-Chief inspected the ship and expressed himself much pleased.

The fleet regatta was held during our stay at Fusan; the sailing regatta took place on Saturday, the 17th, and the rowing races on the following Monday. The sailing races were rather a farce, as the wind, very light at the start, fell to a flat calm after an hour or so, and the boats got round the course simply by persistent "rolling." In the pulling races the China-built boats carried all before them.

Left Fusan on the morning of the 20th, and had a day's steam tactics with the fleet, a final drill, and at last, after night steam tactics, parted company about 10.30 P.M., receiving a shower of civil signals, "pleasant passage," &c., from the other ships, and finally lost sight of the fleet soon after midnight. Thus ended our short but pleasant connection with the China fleet.

The next day was occupied with a steam trial; the weather was hot and sultry, and the coal not of the best; the results were consequently not as good as on a previous occasion.

Draught {	Forward	16 feet
	Aft	20 feet
Steam in boilers		78·3 lbs.
Vacuum {	Forward	25″
	Aft	26″

Revolutions per minute		75·8
Mean Pressure { High		23·4
Low		9·9
Indicated H.P. { High		898·5
Low		1120·2
Total I.H.P.		2018·7
Speed		12·7

The trial was run at natural draught; coal, a mixture of patent fuel and Welsh. Force of the wind about two ahead, and sea fairly smooth. Duration of trial, twelve hours. Engines worked well throughout.

September 22nd.—Encountered the first break of the N.E. monsoon and carried it into Hong-Kong. Through the Formosa Channel it blew very hard, and a considerable sea was running; after passing Amoy thick weather was experienced.

Hong-Kong was reached once more on the morning of September 26th, and the good shelter of the harbour was much appreciated after the big seas outside.

October 1st to 6th.—Leave was given, stores, &c., taken in from the dockyard, and the ship otherwise made ready for the long cruise to Sydney. On October 3rd the ship went into the cosmopolitan dock at Kowloon, in order to repair one of the Kingston valves. Came out of dock on October 6th, and at once began coaling, &c.

The climate of Hong-Kong was found to be much pleasanter in October than in July; although the thermometer only registered 3° or 4° less on the average (in July the highest reading was 91°, and on this occasion 88°), yet the air was much drier and less enervating.

We now heard that on our way to Australia we were to search the Palawan Channel for the missing gunboat

Wasp. The *Wasp* was at this time about a fortnight overdue from Singapore.

Left Hong-Kong on October 7th, and with it said good-bye to the China station, and shaped a course for the Scarborough shoal. The shoal was reached on the 10th, and the ship steered along it on the western side, but without seeing any signs of wreckage. For a large majority on board this was the first sight of coral, and excited much interest. The ring of coral rose in many parts just above the water and enclosed a lovely calm lake, the water inside being of a peculiar green colour. Proceeded through the Palawan Channel, stopping occasionally to examine drift wood, till, on the 13th, Balabac Strait was reached, and the ship's head turned to the eastward to get into the regular steamer track from China to Sydney.

The line was crossed for the third time on October 18th, in about long. 126° E. The passage through these seas was very uneventful ; the greater part of the way there was a flat calm until a light S.E. trade was picked up about lat. 3° S. Amboyna was passed on October 20th.

During this cruise a very energetic amateur theatrical company began operations, and gave more than one performance, which were much appreciated. Some of the dresses and stage fittings had been procured at Hong-Kong. On the 27th athletic sports were held, and proved a very pleasant break in the monotony of a long cruise.

Entered Torres Straits on the 28th ; passed Cape York, and anchored for the night off Cairncross Island. The first sight of Australia was looked out for with much interest; but the Cape York Peninsula has not much to attract attention; the coast line for the most part is low and uninteresting. Almost opposite Cairncross Island, and close to Orfordness, is Pudding-pan Hill, a remarkable eminence, about 650 feet high, with almost a flat top. In the neighbourhood of this hill a noted Australian explorer, Mr. E. B. Kennedy, was killed by the blacks during his disastrous exploration of the Cape York Peninsula in 1848.

Weighed at daylight on the 29th, and anchored at night off Piper Island. On the night of the 30th anchored off Night Island, and on the 31st off Cape Flinders. On November 1st anchored just before midnight off Lizard Island. After this the navigation became less difficult, and it was no longer necessary to anchor at night. Passed Cooktown on November 2nd, Cape Grafton on November 3rd, and Cape Cleveland and Magnetic Island on November 4th; at night saw a large number of bush fires burning brightly on the hills near the coast. As we got further south the coastline became much bolder and more varied. Passed through the beautiful Whitsunday Passage on November 5th, and got clear of the Barrier Reef on the night of the 6th.

The Great Barrier Reef is perhaps the most remarkable example of coral reefs in the world. It extends from Torres Straits along the eastern coast of Australia for about a thousand miles, with only a few breaks navigable for vessels of any size. The reef runs more or less parallel to the coastline, but the interval between them varies in breadth from twenty to seventy miles. On this reef Captain Cook's vessel, the *Endeavour*, grounded, and was much injured by the jagged coral.

November 8th.—So far we had enjoyed a fair-weather passage, but this was too good to last. On November 8th we had a taste of the well-known "southerly buster," and as we had not sufficient coal on board to steam against it, "lay to." The heavy wind and sea continued through the 9th, the ship standing off and on the land under fore staysail, mizen course, and very easy steam. This continued till noon on the 11th, when course was again shaped for Sydney, which we now thought to reach without further mishap, but on the night of the 12th we again encountered a strong "southerly," and had to "lay to" for another forty-eight hours. The force of the wind during these gales was considered to vary from six to nine.

At last on the evening of the 14th the weather moderated, and we once more headed for Sydney, now only about eighty miles distant.

The Australian Station.

After so much provoking delay and bad weather, it seemed almost too good to be true, when, on the morning of the 15th, we found ourselves only a few miles from Sydney Heads, the sea perfectly calm, and the sun shining brightly. Passed Sydney North Head about 10.30 A.M. and made fast to a buoy in Farm Cove before noon.

Every one was on deck as we steamed slowly up Port Jackson to see the harbour of which report spoke so favourably, and certainly the reality quite fulfilled expectation. The entrance is about one and three-quarter miles wide between the Outer, North, and South Heads, narrowing to three-quarters of a mile between the Inner

Heads. The city of Sydney is situated about six miles
from the entrance; a great part of it is built on the
numerous promontories formed by the bays and coves
of the harbour, for, strictly speaking, Port Jackson is
not one harbour, but a collection of harbours; in addition
to the main harbour and channel there are numerous
bays and indentations which afford excellent anchorage
for shipping, and whose united coastline exceeds 160
miles. Shortly after entering Port Jackson we passed
a pleasure steamer full of school-children, who cheered
lustily, and sang "God save the Queen," as a welcome
to the new ship—a kindly English greeting which was
much appreciated.

The only man-of-war in Farm Cove on our arrival
was the *Diamond*. Her ship's company, knowing well
what long cruises and no fresh provisions meant, very
thoughtfully at once sent fresh meat, bread, and vegetables to the messes on the lower deck; the kindness
was suitably acknowledged by inviting the " Diamonds "
to witness a theatrical performance in the evening.

A good understanding was at once set up between the
two ships, and the *Diamond* remained our "chummy
ship" until she left the station.

Amongst the very first to come on board was Mr. J.
S. Shearston, the indefatigable seamen's missionary for
Port Jackson, whose name soon became a household
word in the ship. Mr. Shearston has been working for
many years most successfully among the merchant seamen of the port, and since he undertook the management of the " Goodenough Royal Naval Home," his
work among men of the Royal Navy has been even
more successful. He spares himself no pains or trouble

in order to seek the welfare of the men, and they soon
come to look upon him as their friend.

A few days after our arrival Mr. Shearston organized
an excursion to the Blue Mountains for men on general
leave. A goodly number availed themselves of this
opportunity of seeing something of the neighbourhood,
and an enjoyable day was spent in a visit to the
Wentworth Falls, one of the prettiest spots in the whole
range.

The Blue Mountains form part of the great dividing
range, which runs with scarcely a break of any importance from Cape York on the north to Wilson's Promontory on the south, and forms the watershed between the
rivers which flow into the Pacific and those which run
westward. In most parts of its course the dividing
range is composed of masses of granite and trap, with
rounded or pointed summits. But in the Blue Mountains the prevailing rock is sandstone, which is arranged
in horizontal layers of immense thickness, but broken
up in every direction by vast chasms and ravines with
precipitous sides. The valleys and hillsides are covered
with the universal blue gum, and although the want
of variety in foliage is monotonous, yet the wonderful
blue tints in the distance, and the varying lights and
shades, are most beautiful. Looking out from the top
of one of these precipitous cliffs over the wide-spreading
valley beneath, it is not difficult to imagine that once
the waters of the ocean rolled among these hills, and
formed there beautiful havens like Port Jackson at the
present day. To any one who is not content to say—

"To me are mountain masses grandly dumb ;
I ask not, Whence ? and ask not, Why ? they come,"

the condition of these ranges in former days presents a study of some interest.

There are among the Blue Mountains several water-falls of considerable height, some of them, like Govett's Leap, with a perpendicular drop of over 800 feet; but in all of them, Wentworth Falls included, the volume of water, except after heavy rains, is very small. The hills are approached from Sydney by what is known as the zig-zag railway; and a similar work on a larger scale forms the descent of the western side of the range, and is much talked of as an engineering feat.

There was also plenty to be seen close at hand : a good many hours could be pleasantly spent in visiting the Royal Mint, the Art Gallery in the Domain, the beautiful Botanical Gardens which edge the shores of Farm Cove, and make it as pretty an anchorage as could be wished for, and further afield Coogee Bay, Bondi, and Manly Beach.

Very shortly after arrival the *Calliope* was converted from a white into a black ship, and her appearance much improved by the change.

On November 23rd Lord Carrington, the popular Governor of New South Wales, and the premier, Sir Henry Parkes, visited the ship.

On the 27th, the flag-ship, H.M.S. *Nelson*, with Rear-Admiral Fairfax, C.B., Commander-in-Chief, on board, arrived from Melbourne. The following evening a temperance meeting was held in the torpedo flat, when Mr. Shearston gave a stirring address on the subject of temperance in the navy.

December 16*th*.—After a very pleasant month in Farm Cove, during which much hospitality had been shown to everybody fore and aft, and many acquaintanceships begun which ere long ripened into friendships, the time came to weigh anchor once more, and on December 16th we left for New Zealand. The flag-ship and *Diamond* had started some days earlier. The evening before sailing the *Calliope* theatrical company gave another performance, to which a number of friends from the shore were invited.

24th.—Arrived at Russell, Bay of Islands, about 10 A.M., and at 11 A.M. proceeded about four miles up the harbour to Opua, to take in 100 tons of coal.

The Bay of Islands is a beautiful indentation well protected from the gales of the Pacific by the numerous islands from which it derives its name. Russell, now a quiet little place containing about 250 or 300 inhabitants, was formerly of much greater importance than at present; it was the place first selected as the seat of government when New Zealand became a dependency of the British Crown, and saw stirring times during the Maori War; its original name was Kororareka. The little village of Waitangi, also situated on the Bay of Islands, is noted as the place where the Maori chief in 1840 concluded a treaty by which the sovereignty of the Queen was acknowledged. Coaling was speedily got through, as the ship went alongside a wharf, and the coal was brought down in trucks which were tilted at the right moment and shot the coal on to the deck. After coaling, anchored off Russell about 5.30 P M. Taking in 100 tons of coal was a poor preparation for Christmas, but every effort was made to get the ship clean and presentable by Christmas morning.

D

As Christmas-Day fell on a Sunday it was spent
quietly. The following day was kept as a holiday instead.
A cricket match, Officers *v.* Men, which was played on an
uneven piece of ground surrounded by furze bushes, was
carried to a successful conclusion in spite of local
difficulties, while others organized a seining party in
another part of the bay. The next few days were fully
occupied with target practice of all sorts, and prize
firing. Sailed for Auckland about 6 P.M. on the 30th,
and arrived at our destination about 2 P.M. on the last
day of the year. Here we joined the squadron, consisting of the *Nelson, Diamond, Opal, Rapid,* and *Swinger.*

Numerous excursion steamers were cruising about
till long past midnight, affording their passengers an
opportunity of seeing the old year out amid the
romantic surroundings of the harbour by moonlight.

1888.

January 1st.—Auckland, one of the earliest English settlements in New Zealand, and for long the capital, is still the most populous town in the colony. The city is situated on the south side of the Waitemata Harbour, the numerous branches of which extend far inland. The waters are of sufficient depth to allow of the largest vessels entering the port, and there are practically unlimited facilities for the formation of wharves. Auckland has not many fine buildings either public or private, but it enjoys a most delightful situation. From the higher parts of the city the view of the harbour, with its bays and promontories, and of the island-studded Hauraki Gulf is very fine. The population of Auckland with its suburbs is very nearly 60,000. There is a good Public Library, a good beginning of an Art Gallery and Museum, and a very picturesque recreation ground, named the Domain.

For the first two days of our stay Auckland seemed a pleasure-city rather than an important commercial centre. All shops were shut until January 3rd, and every one seemed bent on getting a real holiday. The district is very evidently of volcanic origin ; a large number of extinct volcanoes are a noticeable feature in

the landscape ; the most prominent of these are Mount
Eden and " One Tree Hill," each about 600 feet high,
and from which a very fine view is to be obtained of the
Waitemata Harbour, Auckland, and the pretty suburb
of Remuera on the eastern side, and on the western
side the little town of Onehunga, and Manakau
Harbour, which is only separated from the Waitemata
by a few miles of solid land.

The fleet sailing regatta took place on January 4th ;
our second cutter and sailing pinnace came in first and
third respectively, each taking the prize for her class.

January 5th.—Sailed for the southward in company
with the fleet and arrived at Wellington about noon on
the 9th, and anchored off the town about half a mile
from the shore. Port Nicholson, the harbour of
Wellington, is a large expanse of water about twelve
miles long by five or six broad, with a narrow entrance.
It is surrounded by lofty hills. Wellington is noted for
its strong winds ; it is nearly always blowing half a gale
there.

Wellington received its first batch of settlers in 1840,
and since 1865 has been the seat of government ; the
population is nearly 20,000. The houses are for the
most part built of wood, as a precaution against earthquakes. Some of these wooden houses are first-rate
imitations of stone structures, and others, without any
pretence of being more substantial than they really are,
are very picturesque. About ten miles from Wellington,
at the other end of the harbour, is the little village of
Lower Hutt, where there are some very pretty houses.
Long to be remembered by lovers of fruit is a tea
garden, full of all kinds of rare plants which were

gathered together by a former owner, but whose present attraction arises from the abundance of strawberries, grapes, &c. At Petone, between Wellington and Lower Hutt, a large establishment for tinning and freezing meat, and a flourishing woollen factory well repay the trouble of a visit. A pleasant day's excursion can also be made to the inland town of Masterton, about seventy miles from Wellington. The railway after passing Lower Hutt surmounts a high range of wooded hills, and descends by steep gradients to the level country beyond. At one point the line is much exposed to violent gusts of wind, sweeping down a valley, and trains have more than once been blown off the line. One such accident occurred shortly after our visit.

One of the things " to do " at Wellington was to walk or ride to Island Bay, about three miles from the town, and pay a visit to the Hermit, an eccentric individual who, for some reason best known to himself, chose to live quite alone in a cave under the cliffs, and declined to tell his name or give his reasons, though he was not averse to conversation on other subjects.

On January 14th the *Calliope* theatrical company gave a successful performance at the little theatre on shore in aid of the Wellington Hospital.

During our stay both at Auckland and Wellington the ships were simply crowded with visitors, especially on Sundays. On the Sunday spent at Wellington it was estimated that about 5,000 people visited the fleet, of which number very nearly 2,000 must have boarded the *Calliope* in the course of the afternoon.

At both these New Zealand towns the fleet met with the greatest hospitality. The following short extract

from a blue-jacket's journal speaks of the kindness
received at Auckland :—

" Like all our people out here in the southern hemisphere, they seem to think they can never do enough
for a blue-jacket. They will feed you, lodge you, walk
you out, and show you all the places of interest, con-
tinually saying, ' You don't see this in the old country,'
or ' What do you think they would say to that in the
old country ? ' The old country lingers in all their
ideas and thoughts. Of course I don't mean the real
bred and born colonial ; yet even the ' coming nation '
like to have the idea that they are imitating the ' old
country's ' ways, and all would like to visit that lump
of mud situated somewhere underneath their feet, of
which they have heard so much from their fathers and
mothers."

January 15*th.*—Sailed in company with the fleet, and
after a rather stormy passage arrived at Sydney on the
evening of the 24th. The object of this break in the
New Zealand cruise was to enable the fleet to assist at
the celebration of the hundredth anniversary of the
foundation of the colony of New South Wales.

January 26th, 1788, was the birthday of the colony,
when Governor Phillip having fixed on Sydney Cove as
the site of the future settlement, the British flag was
hoisted, and the health of King George III. was toasted
with loyal enthusiasm. January 26th, 1888, was consequently the great day of the centenary. All the ships
were dressed with flags, and a royal salute was fired at
noon in honour of the occasion.

The great event of the day was the opening of the
Centennial Park by Lord Carrington in the presence of

a vast crowd of spectators. This park will soon no doubt be worthy of its name, but on the opening day it was little better than a sandy waste. Great progress, however, has since been made in laying it out.

Other functions connected with the centenary were the unveiling of a fine statue of the Queen, the laying the foundation-stone of new Houses of Parliament, and numerous dinners and receptions.

On the afternoon of Sunday, January 27th, a "United Religious Celebration" in connection with the centenary was held in the Exhibition building. This proved a most interesting service, and was very largely attended. Bishop Barry, Primate of Australia, and the leading Presbyterian, Wesleyan, and Congregationalist ministers in Sydney delivered short addresses. Short prayers were said, and several hymns, in which the immense congregation heartily joined, were sung by a powerful choir.

On January 31st a Sailors' Festival was held in the Exhibition building, and proved a great success. A tea was given to about 1,000 seamen. This large number was made up by about 400 men of the Royal Navy, 400 English merchant seamen, 100 French, and 100 Russians from men-of-war of these nations in the harbour. After tea an interval was allowed for smoke and chat, and then came speeches by Lord Carrington, Admiral Fairfax, and Bishop Barry, followed by an appropriate selection of music and songs. The whole affair proved an immense success.

On the evening of February 1st all the ships in the harbour were illuminated, and a grand display of fireworks on Fort Denison, Fort Macquarie, the Domain, and the north shore, made the whole effect really

brilliant. The Russian corvette *Rynda,* which we had
previously met at Vladivostock, was anchored in
Woolloomooloo Bay, and was very prettily illuminated.

This night of illumination closed the long list of
centennial celebrations which had occupied the week.
Not only Australia, but England also, may well be proud
of the progress made by the colonies in a hundred years.
It is often a subject of conjecture how much longer the
present connection between Australia and the mother
country will last, and there are indeed a certain number
of people who believe in the "cut the tow rope" policy,
and make themselves heard; but side by side with that
is a feeling of loyalty as deep and strong as any which
exists in England. The sentiments of the following
verses by James Brunton Stephens, a Queensland poet,
are undoubtedly shared by many Australians :—

AUSTRALIAN ANTHEM.

Maker of earth and sea,
What shall we render Thee ?
   All ours is Thine—
All that our land doth hold,
Increase of field and fold,
Rich ores and virgin gold—
   Thine—Thine—all Thine.

What can Thy children bring !
What save the voice to sing
   "All things are Thine" ?
What to Thy Throne convey ?
What save the voice to pray
"God bless our land alway,
   This land of Thine " ?

O ! with Thy mighty hand
Guard Thou the Motherland ;
   She too is Thine.

Lead her where honour lies,
We beneath other skies
Still clinging daughterwise,
Hers, yet all Thine.

Britons of ev'ry creed,
Teuton and Celt agreed,
Let us be Thine.
One in all noble fame,
Still be our path the same :
Onward in Freedom's name,
Upward in Thine !

Sailed for New Zealand on February 4th, with the
flag-ship and *Diamond.* Arrived at Russell on the 10th,
and immediately went alongside the wharf at Opua,
preparatory to coaling. While coaling was going on
next day several of the officers went up to Kawa-Kawa
to see the coal-mine. The journey by train occupied
about an hour. Kawa-Kawa is a straggling little town
in the midst of a pretty country. The hills are covered
with trees where they have not been destroyed, and
there are plenty of streams in the valleys. The
mine is a small one, but is said to produce a good
quality of coal. Coal, kauri-gum, and manganese from
a mine near the town are the principal exports of
Russell.

Under way firing all day on the 13th; sailed for
Auckland in the evening, and arrived at that place next
morning at 10 A.M.

The *Calliope* was to take a leading part in the opening of a fine new dock, of which the Auckland people
are justly proud. This dock, named after the old
Calliope, a frigate which formerly was well known in
New Zealand waters, was completed shortly after our

arrival on the Australian station, and on account of her
name the Admiral was requested to allow the present
Calliope to be the first ship to enter the dock. The
opening ceremony took place on February 16th. At
9.30 A.M. we entered the dock, breaking a blue ribbon
stretched across it, and were followed by the *Diamond*,
the dock being sufficiently long to take both ships, with
about ten feet to spare. His Excellency the Governor
declared the dock duly open. There was a public lunch
in a shed adjoining the dock, followed by many speeches.
One speaker caused no little amusement by paying a
somewhat doubtful compliment to the good people of
Auckland when he said that "Auckland was a place
where every prospect pleases and only man is vile."
The ubiquitous photographer was of course on the spot,
and some excellent photographs of the ships in dock
were taken. The Calliope Dock has a depth of thirty-
three feet over the sill at low water springs; it is 460
feet long on the blocks, and 525 feet over all; the
breadth of entrance is sixty-two feet. It is certainly
likely to more than provide for all the needs of the port
for some time to come.

The Calliope Dock is situated on the north shore of
Waitemata Harbour, close to the suburb of Devonport.
About four miles from Devonport is Lake Takapuna, a
favourite resort of excursionists. This lake is of immense
depth, and according to the local Maori tradition, the
island of Rangitoto at the entrance of the harbour was
thrown out of it. This statement, however, should be
taken with a grain of salt.

Other things worth seeing in the immediate neighbourhood of Auckland are the beautiful Waitakerei

Falls, and the ostrich farm, each within easy distance for a day's excursion.

For those who have the time to spare a visit to the hot lake district is most interesting. This strange country has of course lost its greatest charm since the destruction of the famous pink and white terraces, but still it remains a weird and interesting region. The coach road from Oxford to Ohinemutu runs for thirty miles through beautiful New Zealand bush, and from Ohinemutu, the little watering place on the banks of Lake Rotorua, an interesting excursion can be made to Wairoa, the Maori village buried by the eruption, or across Lake Tarawera, either to the site of the lost terraces, or up the still smouldering volcano, Tarawera. From the summit a very fine view is obtained over the whole lake district, while far away out at sea White Island throws up a cloud of vapour.

At Wairoa the spot is still pointed out where the aged Maori, Tohutu, whom the natives supposed to have had some hand in causing the disasters, was buried alive under volcanic *débris* during the eruption of Tarawera, on June 10th, 1886, and from which he was rescued after three days.

About three miles from Ohinemutu in another direction is an interesting Maori village named Whaka-rewa-rewa, where there are geysers of considerable size. Here a natural oven can be obtained by simply digging a hole in the ground and placing in it whatever is to be cooked, when the heat is sufficient to produce the required effect. The little Maori children at Whaka-rewa-rewa do not trouble their heads about school boards or examinations, but sit all day long up to

their necks in the warm pools, and are ready to dive
for the coppers which visitors are beguiled into throwing to them.

The Sailors' Home at Auckland is a handsome new
building about four minutes' walk from the landing-
place. At first it did not find much favour with our
men, but on our next visit, when some alterations had
been made in the management, it was well liked.

On February 27th athletic sports for the officers and
men of the fleet were held in the Domain, and attracted
a very large number of spectators. The prizes were
provided by the Mayor and Corporation of Auckland,
and many of the events were keenly contested.

Sailed for the southward on February 28th, and
arrived at Port Lyttelton about 4 P.M., on March 3rd,
and anchored in the outer harbour more than two miles
from the town. There is a very snug inner harbour
formed by artificial breakwaters; our draught of water,
however, was unfortunately slightly too large to admit
of our going inside, and we were compelled to remain
outside exposed to strong easterly winds and a considerable sea.

Lyttelton in itself is only a small place, population
about 4,500; but it is important as being the port of
Christchurch, and the outlet for the produce of a large
district. Christchurch is now connected with Lyttelton by a railway about eight miles long. The construction of this line was a costly undertaking, as it neces-
sitated a tunnel through a mile and a half of volcanic
rock. The early settlers were obliged to "hump their
swag" over the hills.

Christchurch, the capital of the province of Canterbury, stands on the banks of a small stream called the Avon, in the midst of a fertile plain. It is a prosperous town, well laid out, and has some fine public buildings, including the Government buildings and the museum, the latter is said, probably with truth, to be the finest and best arranged museum in the southern hemisphere. The Church of England cathedral stands on one side of the Central Square. In March, 1888, it had a graceful spire, but forty feet of this has since been thrown down by an earthquake shock which visited the locality and caused considerable injury to buildings. There are several good schools and a university, all of which are said to be in a prosperous condition. The river is spanned by several handsome bridges, and each of these has the name of some past mayor of Christchurch inscribed upon it. These functionaries have certainly chosen a useful as well as an ornamental way of handing their names down to posterity. The population of the city is about 30,000. Christchurch is generally considered to be the most English of all colonial towns, and the impressions received on a flying visit certainly agree with that opinion.

Sailed at 7 A.M. on March 8th, and after rather a rough passage round Banks' Peninsula, arrived at Akaroa about 2 P.M. This is one of the finest harbours in the country; it is a perfect land-locked harbour with anchorage for a considerable number of ships. The little town of Akaroa, containing about 700 inhabitants, consists almost entirely of wooden houses; like most New Zealand towns it has public gardens, of course on a small scale. The surrounding country is very hilly and very fertile. Orchards abound. A quantity of "cocksfoot" grass is grown and exported. Akaroa was originally a French settlement, and one or two of the original settlers are still living in the town.

Sailed at 7 A.M. on March 9th, and arrived off Port Chalmers about 10 A.M. on the 10th, but were obliged to wait for the tide until one o'clock before crossing the bar. As we entered the harbour the water presented a peculiar appearance, being covered with large patches of bright red, occasioned by shoals of small red fish, something the shape of a lobster, and known in these parts as "whale's food." Here again we were obliged to anchor about two miles from the landing-place, but in a more sheltered position than at Lyttelton.

Port Chalmers, on the inlet called Otago Harbour, is the port of Dunedin. It is a place of great trade, and has accommodation for a large quantity of shipping. The aggregate burden of the ships which enter and leave the port annually is about half a million tons.

Dunedin, the capital of the province of Otago, is the second most populous town in New Zealand ; its population, including the suburbs, is about 45,000. The position of the city, on an arm of the sea running inland for about fifteen miles, is charming. Its public buildings are the finest in the colony. The streets are well lighted and well paved, and the trade is extensive. As Christchurch is the most English town in New Zealand, so Dunedin is the most Scotch. The city was named by the original settlers after their own Edinburgh. And at the present day a majority of the inhabitants hail from north of the Tweed.

Vessels of moderate size can come up to the city ; large ones unload at Port Chalmers. During our stay the *Swinger* was alongside a wharf at Dunedin, and was crowded with visitors. We, too, had our full share both at Port Lyttelton and Port Chalmers; though the pleasure they derived from the visit must have been more imaginary than real, as at the former place many of them were sea-sick, and at the latter they were drenched by the heavy showers of rain and hail which came down at frequent intervals.

Sailed for Wellington about 2.30 P.M. on March 14th, had fair winds and calm sea till the morning of the 16th, when the wind drew ahead, and about noon, when we were less than twenty miles from Port Nicholson, it was blowing a gale from the N.W.; the rain and spray were so thick that the land was completely obscured, and we were obliged to run under the lee of Cape Palliser for shelter; the force of the wind during the afternoon and evening varied from eight to ten.

On the morning of the 17th the weather moderated, and we anchored off Wellington at 4 P.M. We remained at Wellington till noon on the 22nd, when we sailed for Nelson, arriving at that place about noon on the following day.

Nelson is a charming little town of about 7,000 inhabitants, situated near the head of Tasman Bay. The harbour is unfortunately shallow, and we were obliged to anchor in the bay about three miles from the town. Nelson is rarely visited by a man-of-war, and in consequence many of the people were anxious to see the ship, and a large number came off in a steamer, but on account of the heavy sea they were not able to come alongside, and had to content themselves with steaming round the ship. The town has a few indus-

tries, but is an extremely quiet little place, quite a
"sleepy hollow"; having no railway communication,
and only accessible from Wellington by a line of coast-
ing steamers, it seems almost cut off from the outside
world.   Nearly all the buildings are of wood ; on the
outskirts of the town are many very pretty wooden
villas, standing in charming gardens, full of all kinds of
flowers and shrubs.   Nelson is said to be the healthiest
place in New Zealand, and that is saying a good deal.

On the following day we sailed for Sydney: the
passage was a pleasant one but longer than had been
anticipated, as during the last two days a very strong
adverse current (100 miles in forty-eight hours) was
experienced.   Arrived at Sydney about 6 A.M. on
April 2nd, and as all the buoys in Farm Cove were
in use, anchored off Garden Island in Woolloomooloo
Bay.

On April 8th H.M.S. *Thalia* and *Egeria* arrived, the
former with relief crews for the *Rapid* and *Myrmidon.*

About 1.30 P.M. on April 14th, we sailed for Fiji *viâ*
Norfolk Island.   On the morning of the 17th we passed
between Lord Howe Island and Ball's Pyramid.

Arrived at Norfolk Island about 9 A.M. on April 20th.
This island was the first of all the Pacific islands to be
definitely settled by white men.   It was discovered by
Captain Cook in 1774, and in February, 1788, Lieutenant Philip Gidley King, afterwards the third Governor
of New South Wales, was sent to found a penal settlement on Norfolk Island in connection with the colony
recently founded at Port Jackson.   This penal settlement continued to exist on the island, with one short
exception in 1805, for sixty-seven years, and was the

place of confinement of the most desperate criminals;
but in 1855 the convict establishment was finally
abandoned.

In 1856 the inhabitants of Pitcairn Island, the
descendants of the *Bounty* mutineers, were removed
from their own small island, which had become insuffi-
cient for their augmented numbers, and were settled
on Norfolk Island, where they have lived ever since,
with few changes in the manners and customs of their
little community. There are strict regulations restricting
the settlement of outsiders in the island; the only
important exception to these rules has been the establishment of the head-quarters of the Melanesian
Mission, in 1866, when 1,000 acres of land were bought
from the islanders for the use of the mission.

There is no sheltered anchorage near Norfolk Island,
but there are two landing-places, one in Sydney Bay,
on the south side of the island, which is close to the
old convict prison, and is generally used when possible;
and the other in Cascade Bay, on the N.E. side, which
is often available when a heavy southerly swell makes
the former place impracticable.

On the present occasion the ship anchored in Sydney
Bay. As soon as we were anchored we were boarded
by Bishop Selwyn, the head of the Melanesian Mission,
and Mr. Nobbs, one of the leaders of the Norfolk
Island colony, who came off in a whale boat manned by
four stalwart islanders. The Bishop most kindly invited
as many officers as could do so to land with him, and
see as much of the island and the mission as the short
time at our disposal allowed. Even on a moderately
calm day the landing is rather exciting to the inex-

E

perienced, as the boat rises over the large waves on her
way through the narrow channel in the reef, and then
at once finds herself in calm water close alongside the
little stone pier. Quite a crowd was collected on the
shore to have a look at the visitors ; there were men of
all ages, women young and old, and any number of
children ; amongst them, too, was the oldest man in the
island —— Buffett, born in 1797. He was not one of
the *Bounty* mutineers, but one of the crew of a whaler
which touched at Pitcairn Island, when Buffett elected
to join the little colony.

There was just time for a rapid look through the
ruins of the old prison buildings, sombre memorials of
a state of things which happily has passed away, and
then an hour or so remained for a visit to the mission
before returning to the ship. The mission is situated
in the centre of the island, and is reached by a fine
road between an avenue of the splendid pines for which
Norfolk Island is famous. The establishment consists
of six or seven houses where the missionaries live with
their pupils, a large dining-hall where all take their
meals in common, a number of school-rooms, printing-
shop, carpenters' and blacksmiths' shops, &c., and in a
central situation the beautiful church built in memory
of Bishop Patteson, first Bishop of Melanesia, who was
killed at Santa Cruz in 1871. The plan of the mission
is to bring native boys and girls from the Melanesian
islands, to Norfolk Island, and when they have been
carefully trained and taught, then they are sent back
to their own islands, and exercise a very wide civilizing
and Christianizing influence.

After receiving much kindness and hospitality from

the Bishop and Mrs. Selwyn we returned to the ship, and sailed at 1.30 P.M.

About 10 A.M. on April 27th we arrived at Suva, the present capital of Fiji. We were delayed for nearly half an hour outside the harbour by heavy rain, which quite obscured the leading marks. Suva Harbour is a fine bay, sheltered on the north by the land, and on the south is quite protected from the sea by the reef. The Fiji group consists of about 250 islands, of which only about seventy are inhabited. The two principal islands are Viti Levu (Great Fiji), and Vanua Levu (Great Land). Coral reefs fringe almost all the islands and add greatly to the intricacy of the navigation. Tasman, the great Dutch navigator, first discovered these islands in 1646, but after that they remained unnoticed till visited by Captain Cook, more than a hundred years later. They were annexed to the British Crown in 1874, when Sir Arthur Gordon became first Governor.

The total population of Fiji at the present time is about 128,000, of whom only about 3,500 are European colonists ; 115,000 are native Fijians and the remainder are immigrants from India and Polynesia. Suva is a straggling little town with about 500 European inhabitants. The Government Offices are the most noticeable buildings in the town, and the Governor's house is prettily situated about a mile from the centre of the town. The roads are very bad ; there is, in fact, only one road leading into the interior, and even this after a few miles becomes little more than a track. From the high ground behind the town a very fine view is obtained of the valley of the Rewa, the largest river in Fiji, and the highway of an important district. On its

banks is a large sugar mill, said to be the largest establishment of the kind in the world. We were sent to
Fiji on this occasion in order to convey the Governor,
Sir John Bates Thurston, K.C.M.G., to open the annual
Parliament of native chiefs. This parliament, which is
called " Vei Bose Vaka Turanga," that is, the " Council
of Chiefs," is held in different islands in the group
every year. This year the place of meeting was the
small island of Ngau, in the district named " Lomai
Viti " (heart of Fiji).

Early on the morning of May 1st, his Excellency the
Governor, with his private secretary and also the editor
of the *Fiji Times*, and Ratu Abel, the leading Fijian
chief, son of the late King Thakombau, came on board
for passage to Ngau. Arrived at Ngau about 3 P.M.
the same day. The entrance to the harbour is narrow,
and the only leading mark the peak of a hill on a line
with the centre of a sandy beach ; as this is a somewhat
vague direction, while the coral reefs are dangerous
neighbours, a small Government steamer, which had
brought over the interpreters and other officials, came
outside to point out the way in. Immediately on arrival
four native chiefs came off to pay their respects to the
Governor, who received them on the poop. These
natives presented a strange appearance as they came
over the side, for they were enveloped in immense rolls
of tappa, the native cloth, from which they unwound
themselves at the close of the ceremony and which they
left on the deck with whales'-teeth and other gifts.

The following day, May 2nd, the great ceremonies
began. About eleven his Excellency the Governor left
the ship, attended by Captain Kane, Lieutenant Carter,

and Lieutenant Marchant, in full uniform. Yards were manned, and a salute of seventeen guns fired. As many officers as could leave the ship also landed to attend the ceremony ; and later, special leave was given to the port watch. On approaching the shore we saw a number of Fijians standing up to their shoulders in the shallow water, to mark the channel for the Governor's boat. These living buoys were a curious and novel sight. The proceedings began with a " meki " or ceremonial dance: as soon as this was over every one adjourned to the council-chamber, a large hut in the centre of an open square.

The Governor and his staff and the English visitors were seated at one end, while the body of the room was occupied by Fijian chiefs of the different orders, seated on the ground. The titles of these chiefs are two; the higher is Roko-tui, *i.e.*, governor of a province; the inferior is Buli, the governor of a district under the Roko-tui. Every chief has also the title " Ratu," corresponding perhaps, to " Lord " or " Sir." The proceedings began with a prayer by a native Fijian minister. This was followed by the ceremonial making and drinking of " kava," or, as it is called in Fiji " yangona," a most solemn proceeding. Then followed the Governor's speech, which he delivered in English on account of the number of visitors present, and which was translated by the interpreter. The Governor's commission and a letter from the Queen were also read. In his speech the Governor suggested several topics of discussion for the Bose ; referred to the events of the past year, and distributed praise or rebuke to those chiefs who deserved encouragement or warning. One chief who had been

on probation for a year, was installed as Roko-tui ; and
another named Ratu-Beni, who was similarly on probation, was kept in the lower rank for another year on
account of certain delinquencies; the crowning fault
was that he had brought as many as 160 followers to
Ngau on this occasion, when the number was strictly
limited to twenty.

After the speeches and installations were over,
more " mekis " were gone through with much vigour
both by women and men. The men's "meki" was a
wild-looking war-dance; the warriors were in full dress,
their faces painted hideous colours, and armed with
formidable-looking clubs and spears.

On May 3rd the Rokos and Bulis were invited to
come on board to see the ship. They came in large
numbers, and seemed much interested by all they saw.
A mine was exploded (Ratu Abel touching the key), and
caused great excitement. The firing of the Nordenfelts
also called forth loud applause, and the marines' bayonet
exercise was evidently considered a good "meki."

Weighed anchor at noon, and had a quick run across to
Ovalau, arriving at Levuka soon after three. Ovalau is
a small, mountainous island, close to the eastern side of
Viti Levu; its one town is Levuka, formerly the capital
of Fiji, and which has declined in importance since the
seat of Government was removed to Suva. Levuka is
prettily situated between high, richly-wooded hills and
the sea; its situation suggests reminiscences of Hong-
Kong.

We were to convey Sir John Thurston to Samoa in
his capacity of High Commissioner of the Western
Pacific; and on the morning of the 5th, the acting

Chief Justice of Fiji, and the secretary to the High Commissioner came on board. Sailed for Samoa at 9 A.M.

Arrived at Apia about noon on May 9th, after a calm passage. The Samoan, or as it was formerly called, the Navigator group, has three principal islands—Savai, Upolu, and Tutuila. Of these although Savai is the largest, yet Upolu is of most commercial importance, and contains the capital, Apia, where a considerable number of Europeans reside. The harbour is a very poor one ; ships lie in the opening of the reef and are quite exposed to any northerly wind and sea. And at times, even when quite calm, a most unpleasant swell sets in, causing the ship to roll heavily ; and in consequence, all lower deck scuttles have to be closed, which is no slight inconvenience when the thermometer stands at 86° or 87° F.

We found in harbour the United States corvette *Mohican,* and the German gun-vessel *Adler.* The scenery round Apia is very beautiful. The island is hilly and wonderfully fertile ; it is a great place for fruit—oranges, cocoa-nuts, limes, bananas, mangoes, and alligator-pears are most abundant. The residence of the native king of Samoa is about a mile and a half from Apia on Mulinu Point. The present king, Tamasese, is supported by the Germans, who deposed the former king, Malietoa, and transported him to the Cameroons. At 2 P.M. on May 13th, sailed for Ngau, where the Governor was going to close the Bose.

We arrived at Ngau on the 17th, and next day the Governor closed the Bose. This was accompanied by many "mekis" and by a vast amount of present-giving. Enormous piles of cocoa-nut matting, tappa, bottles of cocoa-nut oil, and whales' teeth, were heaped in the

middle of the square by long lines of natives who filed
past, each adding his contribution to the heap.

It seemed to be etiquette to throw the present down
with a careless gesture, as if it were the most worthless
thing in the world. The presents most highly prized
were whales' teeth. As each tooth was flung down it
was greeted with a shout of " venaka, venaka " (good,
good), and by emphatic grunts of approval. All these
valuables were nominally presents to the Governor.
As a matter of fact however they were all returned and
redistributed among the different tribes.

Sailed for Suva at 9 A.M. on May 19th, and arrived
there shortly after 3 P.M. The Governor, and the rest
of our passengers went on shore at once.

It is impossible to get any idea of the mode of life
of the natives in Suva itself, but about four miles out, at
Tama-vua, which can be reached either by road or by
boat up a pretty little river, a real native village can be
seen. The houses are dark, and the whole appearance
rather dirty, but in this respect it is said not to be a
fair specimen of a Fijian village.

May 24th.—On the Queen's Birthday dressed ship
and fired salute at noon. In the afternoon the *Calliope*
cricket team played a match *v.* Suva, and suffered
defeat, after a very good game. The match was played
on the " rara," or parade ground of the armed native
constabulary, close to Government House. The grounds
of Government House are well stocked with all kinds
of beautiful and useful plants : and in some half-wild
botanical gardens on the other side of the town are a
great number of valuable tropical plants, which have
been collected there by Sir John Thurston.

Under way, running torpedoes in the forenoon of the 28th. Sailed for the Great Astrolabe Reef in the afternoon. Carried out machine-gun prize firing by night, and next morning anchored inside the reef off the island of Kandava. The 30th was occupied with prize-firing. We cleared the reef before dark and anchored in Suva Harbour about midnight.

Suva is a very rainy place. Heavy rain fell almost every day during our stay : but an exceptional fall took place on June 1st, when eight and a quarter inches were registered between 8 A.M. and 1 P.M. This is the heaviest fall since a record has been kept.

Sailed for Sydney at 4 P.M. on June 2nd. Encountered a series of head winds, and in consequence put into Noumea for coal on the 9th. We ran along for ten or twelve miles in the smooth water inside the coral reef before reaching the entrance to the harbour, and finally through a narrow, but not difficult passage between hilly islands steamed into a perfectly sheltered harbour which affords good anchorage for a large number of ships.

Noumea is the capital of the French colony of New Caledonia, and the headquarters of the large convict establishments in that island. The town is well laid out; fairly wide, straight streets at right angles to one another cover the level ground, much of which has been reclaimed, between the sea and the hills behind the town, but the houses with few exceptions are mean-looking. Many of the streets have now avenues of trees which are beginning to make some progress. There is a pretty square, La Place de Cocotiers, where the convict band plays three times a week, and near this is a recreation ground where some of the residents indulge in lawn tennis and cricket.

The harbour abounds with fish, and some very good sport can be obtained by any one who cares to take a little trouble over the matter. The climate is very pleasant during the greater part of the year, but in January and February it is very hot. Convicts and *libérés* are to be seen everywhere; the place in fact would be nothing without the convicts : they have made the excellent roads which contrast very favourably with the wretched roads at Suva, and their constant attempts at escape form an unceasing source of local excitement.

Coaled on the 11th, and at 7 A.M. on the 12th sailed for Sydney.

A twelve hours' full speed trial took place on June 18th, when an average of 13·1 knots was obtained. Arrived at Sydney about 11 A.M. on June 19th, when five weeks' mails were brought on board, and provided ample reading for the next few days. A month in Farm Cove within reach of the many attractions of Sydney was a pleasant change after an island cruise. During this time general leave was given, the ship provisioned and coaled, the moorings examined, the ship's company went through annual course of musketry instruction, and a blue-jacket battalion was landed for drill preparatory to taking part in the ceremony of opening the Exhibition at Melbourne.

On the evening of June 27th Mr. Shearston gave a temperance address, illustrated by magic-lantern slides, on the lower deck.

Sailed for Melbourne at 10 A.M. on July 21st, with the *Nelson, Diamond, Rapid* and *Lizard.* This proved a rough and uncomfortable passage. At starting we had a light wind from the N.W., but during the afternoon a heavy squall came on, and nearly every ship lost one or more sails. The barometer began to fall rapidly, and there were frequent heavy squalls during the night. After rounding Gabo Island we encountered strong head gales and a heavy sea. Most of the ships lost spars. The *Diamond* and *Rapid* each lost their stern boat; and the *Rapid* was obliged to ease down as she was being washed fore and aft, when driven against such a sea. By the time Wilson's Promontory was abeam, the wind was going down and the barometer rising.

About 1 A.M., on July 26th, we anchored on the quarantine ground, inside Port Phillip Head: the *Rapid* arrived about 7 A.M., and an hour or so later the squadron weighed and proceeded up Port Phillip towards Hobson's Bay, where we anchored off Williamstown, about 4 P.M. The mouth of the river Yarra is at the north-west corner of Hobson's Bay, and is navigable for ships drawing less than fifteen feet up to the wharves at Melbourne; large sailing ships go alongside wharves at Port Melbourne (formerly called Sandridge), and the mail steamers alongside the railway pier at Williamstown, which is connected with the city of Melbourne by a line of rail running for six and a half miles through a flat, uninteresting country, thickly dotted with poor-looking houses. Entering Melbourne on this side, you see it at its worst; but the regular streets and fine buildings of the city soon remove the feeling of disappointment produced by the journey through the suburbs. The growth of Melbourne has been even more rapid than that of Sydney; founded in 1836, it now contains, with its suburbs, more than 400,000 inhabitants. The cable-trams which run through the principal streets are a comfortable and expeditious mode of locomotion, and are a vast improvement on the Sydney steam-trams. The people of Victoria have been lavish in their expenditure on public buildings; the Government Offices, the Town-hall, and the Post-office are all fine buildings, but will be quite eclipsed by the New Parliament House, which is at present in course of construction, and, according to the plans, will be a magnificent building.

There are many other objects of interest in Melbourne and its neighbourhood. The Botanical Gardens, and the Observatory, well repay the trouble of a visit; and in another direction the Museum, Art Gallery, and Public Library afford interesting occupation for many an hour. The library is an exceptionally good one, and is contained in a handsome building where every arrangement is made for the convenience of readers.

The Centennial Exhibition was opened on August 1st by Sir Henry B. Loch, G.C.M.G., Governor of Victoria. A battalion was landed from the fleet to form part of the troops lining the streets through which the Governor, accompanied by Admiral Fairfax and the Governors of the other Australasian colonies, were to pass on their way to the Exhibition building.

The streets were thronged with thousands of people eager to see the procession pass. The ceremony inside the building opened with prayer, followed by speeches appropriate to the occasion. The National Anthem, and an ode composed by an Australian poet, were beautifully rendered by a powerful choir and orchestra, which had been perfectly trained by Mr. Cowen.

Although the Exhibition was now formally opened, yet it was still very far from complete; many of the exhibits were still unpacked, it was therefore impossible to judge of it as a whole, but as far as could be judged it bade fair to be full of interest. The most notable, and most entirely successful parts of the Exhibition, were undoubtedly the fine collection of pictures, particularly the English and German galleries, and the very fine series of instrumental and vocal concerts, which were held at frequent intervals during the time the Exhibition was open. The next few days were a time of great festivity in Melbourne, and the officers of the fleet came in for their full share of hospitality.

Banquets were given in the Exhibition building, and in the Town hall. Two balls were given at Government House, at each of which about 2,000 people were present, and which were very brilliant affairs.

After an exceedingly pleasant stay, the fleet sailed for Sydney on August 11th. Shortly after weighing, the flag-ship took the ground, but after a short delay she was towed off by the *Calliope*.

Reached Sydney on the 14th, and moored in Woolloomooloo Bay. Employed refitting and giving leave.

H.M.S. *Orlando*, the new flag-ship, arrived on August 26th, to relieve the *Nelson*.

August 27th the Commander-in-Chief came on board to inspect the ship. Everything went off in a most satisfactory manner.

Admiral Fairfax hoisted his flag in the *Orlando* at 8 A.M. on September 1st. On the same day H.M.S.

Diamond, whose time was up on the station, left for England *viâ* Auckland, at which port she was to wait until her relief, the *Royalist*, daily expected from the Cape station, should arrive at Albany.

As she steamed out of Farm Cove she received the customary farewell cheers from the other ships of the squadron, and from none more heartily than from the *Calliope*. The *Diamond* had also been a great favourite with the Sydney watermen, who now combined to give her a good " send-off," forming a long procession of boats adorned with flags, which accompanied her part of the way down the harbour.

On September 3rd the old flag-ship sailed for England and received a hearty " send-off," large crowds of people assembling on Man-of-War Steps, and in the Domain, to wave a farewell to their friends.

On the afternoon of September 4th Admiral Fairfax hoisted his flag in the *Calliope*, and about 5 P.M., in company with the *Lizard*, we proceeded to sea, bound on a cruise among the islands.

About 9 A.M., on September 7th we arrived off Lord Howe Island. The Admiral and a few of the officers landed, the ship in the meanwhile remaining under way off the island. Lord Howe Island is a pretty hilly little island, and very fertile ; it contains about six-and-thirty inhabitants. There is no regular communication with Australia, but vessels occasionally touch at it *en route* to Norfolk Island or Fiji. Sailed about noon.

Reached Norfolk Island on September 10th, about 5 P.M. A boat at once came off from the shore, but as it was blowing very fresh the landing was difficult

in Sydney Bay, and we towed the boat round to Cascade
Bay, where they were able to effect a landing. The ship
remained under way off the island during the night,
and next morning the Admiral landed in Cascade Bay,
and the ship went round to Sydney Bay, where the
landing was now fairly easy. In the afternoon several
officers landed and visited the ruined prison and the
mission. Bishop Selwyn was at this time absent on
a missionary cruise among the Melanesian islands, but
Mrs. Selwyn and several of the mission staff did the
honours of the mission station.

All on board again soon after four and sailed at once
for Tonga. We noticed several whalers cruising off
Norfolk Island; these ships, from time to time, land
their men for a run on the island : and a number of the
Norfolk Islanders serve for a time as seamen on board.

Arrived at Tongatabu (sacred Tonga) about 11 A.M.
on the 19th. The Tonga Islands, also called the
Friendly Islands, are about 390 miles E.S.E. of Fiji.
They include three groups of islands, Tongatabu,
Haapai, and Vavau; the total area is about 385 square
miles, and the population 21,000. Tongatabu is a
thorough coral island; it is very flat, covered with
luxuriant vegetation and surrounded by coral reefs.
The little town of Nukalufa faces the harbour; it consists chiefly of native huts, but there are some buildings
of greater pretensions ; amongst these may be mentioned
the residence of King George of Tonga, a building
after the style of a suburban villa, only built of wood ;
close to this is a very pretty little wooden church with
two small spires, the interior very neatly fitted up with
kauri pine from New Zealand. The Wesleyan Mission

House is also a prominent object, and on a small hill, about 100 feet high behind, the town, stands a long low building with thatched roof beautifully made in Tongan fashion, which is the old church and school-room of the Wesleyan Mission. Shortly after arrival we saluted the Tongan flag with twenty-one guns; the salute was returned by a battery on shore.

This little battery consisted of eight or ten old guns of different patterns, mostly three-pounders and six-pounders, which had probably been supplied by some enterprising trader. The manner in which the salute was fired caused much amusement. It was raining heavily at the time, and in consequence a Tongan soldier held an umbrella carefully over each touch-hole to keep the powder dry, and the guns were fired by what looked like a red hot poker brought hurriedly from a fire which was burning close at hand.

The Tongans are a fine race, intellectually and physically; they, like the Maoris and the Samoans, are vastly superior to the people of the New Hebrides, New Caledonia, or the Solomon Islands, while the Fijians occupy an intermediate position. A Wesleyan mission has for many years been established in Tonga, which may now be considered as a Christian country; this mission was for long one of the most successful of the missions among the Pacific islands; but of late years a most unfortunate division has arisen between the original Wesleyan Mission and what is known as the Tongan Free Church, which was founded through the agency of Mr. Baker, formerly a Wesleyan missionary, and now the chief adviser of King George, and practically the ruler of Tonga.

The course of study in the Government schools is very comprehensive ; more so almost than seems needful. There are numerous broad grass roads in the island, which are very good indeed in dry weather, but very soft after rain. About fourteen miles from Nukalufa are some curious caves, said to extend for two miles or more ; only about sixty or seventy yards of them, however, can be seen without wading or swimming through pools of water.

On September 24th King George of Tonga, accompanied by Mr. Baker, visited the ship ; yards were manned and a salute of twenty-one guns fired.

H.M.S. *Egeria* was in harbour during our stay. A strange accident befell our ward-room skiff one evening when she was taking half-a-dozen officers to a "singsong" on board the *Egeria*. It was a pitch-dark night and raining, and when the boat had got fifty or sixty yards from the ship, two of the bottom planks were stove in by some large fish, probably one of the sharks with which the harbour swarms. The skiff at once began to fill, and was with difficulty got alongside the sailing pinnace. All her occupants had a thorough ducking, but were otherwise none the worse for the adventure.

The Tongans are passionately fond of cricket, so much so that the number of days a week on which play is allowed has to be regulated by law, otherwise more important things would be neglected. They play the game very well, excelling especially in bowling and fielding. An eleven of Tongan students defeated an eleven from the ships during our stay. The Tongans have a very great notion of their own importance in the

F

world. An amusing story is told which illustrates this.
At the time of the Franco-German war it is said King
George gravely requested the German Consul to inform
the Emperor that Tonga would remain strictly neutral.

At 4.30 on the 25th we sailed for Vavau, arrived at
our destination on the 27th, and anchored in Port
Valdez about noon. The harbour and its approaches
are the prettiest we have seen as yet in this part of the
world. We passed between a number of small islets
with high perpendicular cliffs, in some cases much
undermined at the water's edge, and anchored in a
narrow channel between high wooded hills, the depth
of water being about twenty fathoms not more than a
cable from the shore on either side. Farther on the
channel widened out considerably, and formed a larger
harbour, but with much less depth of water. The
vegetation on shore was most luxuriant—oranges,
limes, and other fruits to be had for the picking up.

Vavau is famed for its caves. There is one celebrated
cavern whose entrance is under water, and which can
be only reached by an expert diver. This is the cave
of which Byron has given a description in his poem,
The Island ; or, Christian and his Comrades, where he
gives an account of the fate of some of the *Bounty*
mutineers. The poet, however, acknowledges in a note
that he has taken the poetical liberty of transplanting
this cave from Tonga to Tahiti.

We weighed anchor at 7.30 A.M. on the following
morning. On the way out of harbour boats were
lowered to visit a beautiful cave under the high cliffs.
Three boats entered it easily, and it could have contained several more. The deep tints of the water and

strange lights and shades on the walls and roof of the cavern were very beautiful.

At 5 P.M. on September 30th we arrived at Pango-pango in Tutuila, one of the Samoan group. The harbour is completely land-locked; a narrow winding entrance leads into the harbour, which has the appearance of a beautiful inland lake, surrounded by high hills covered with most luxuriant vegetation. Two or three villages are dotted at intervals along the shores of the harbour, but there is no town of any size. Large numbers of canoes surrounded the ship, and some very good clubs and kava-bowls were to be obtained. The natives asked a high price in money; but for an old coat with uniform buttons they were ready to part with almost anything.

The people at Pango-pango have not been thrown so much into contact with Europeans as those at Apia; very few knew any English, but all seemed friendly and well-disposed. The houses were in the same style as those in the neighbourhood of Apia : a beautifully made thatched roof supported on strong posts; the walls formed of mats, which could be rolled up and let down at pleasure; and the floors of shingle with a hollow for the fire in the centre; these, however, did not seem so clean and well kept as in Upolu.

Here we heard that there had been some fighting in the neighbourhood of Apia between the parties of Tamasese and Malietoa.

Sailed at 4 P.M. on October 1st and arrived at Apia the following morning about eleven. There had been some sharp fighting about a fortnight earlier, and there was still considerable excitement. Malietoa's party, under the command of a chief named Mataafa, had attacked Tamasese's men, and driven them from a long line of entrenchments near Matautu Point. The defeated party, retreated to Mulinu Point, and were there shut in, their opponents endeavouring to starve them into submission. The only fighting which took place during our stay was in consequence of attempts to bring food and water in boats from places along the coast, when shots were exchanged between the opposing parties, but little harm was done to either side.

The fortifications, which had been the scene of the recent fighting, consisted of long lines of earth embankments, strengthened with grass bags filled with earth, the whole making a strong defence. Mataafa was living at the time in a village near Matautu Point; he is a fine-looking, dignified old man; his son, who speaks English well, acted as interpreter.

The U.S.S. *Adams* and the German gun-vessel *Adler* were in harbour at the time, protecting American and German interests respectively.

On October 7th the *Nyanza*, a pretty schooner yacht of 218 tons, owned by Captain Cumming Dewar, arrived at Apia on her way round the world. She left Plymouth on July 21st, 1887, and we afterwards heard that she reached Kobe, Japan, on August 8th, 1889.

On October 10th we sailed for Fiji at 4.30 P.M. The *Lizard* remained behind to protect British interests.

Arrived at Taviuni and anchored off Somo-somo shortly before noon on October 14th. There is no good harbour, the water is very deep up to about two cables from the shore, and then shoals rapidly. Taviuni is fourth in size among the islands of the Fiji Group. It is twenty-three miles long and from five to eight broad. The island is of volcanic formation, and capable of cultivation from summit to water-line. It is densely wooded, and there is a large rainfall on the higher ground. Cotton, coffee, sugar, and copra are the chief products. Somo-somo is the residence of Ratu Lala, Roko Tui of the district of Taviuni.

Sailed at 6.30 A.M. on the 15th, and arrived at Suva about midnight.

October 16*th.*—The weather during our stay was far from pleasant, thunderstorms with heavy rain occurring each afternoon. After a short and uneventful stay we left again on the 19th, bound for the New Hebrides.

On the morning of October 23rd we were off Pentecost Island, New Hebrides. The island is hilly and densely wooded. There were no houses to be seen, nor any natives. At 2 P.M. the same day we arrived at Port Sandwich in the island of Mallicolo, sometimes spelt Malekula.

The inhabitants of Mallicolo are not an interesting race; they are noted for their ugliness both of form and feature.

Here we found the schooner *Helena*, of Maryborough, Queensland, engaged in the labour trade; she had just arrived from Ambrym, where, on the previous day, her boat's crew had been fired on by the natives and three men shot. Two, who were dangerously wounded, were brought on board for passage to hospital at Noumea; these were Mr. Heath, mate of the *Helena*, and a seaman named Isaac Osborn.

The French man-of-war *Fabert* arrived on October 24th, and the joint commission met to consider the

case of the *Helena,* but there was not sufficient evidence
forthcoming, and the case was adjourned.

There is no town at Port Sandwich, only a few
traders' houses, and some native villages half hidden
in the bush. These villages were miserable affairs, and
in the daytime almost deserted, nearly all the people
being away at work. The houses were poor and dirty-
looking, and the people the lowest type of human
beings we had yet seen, immeasurably inferior to the
fine Samoans and Tongans.

We sailed for Noumea at 5 P.M. the same day, in-
tending to call at only two other islands in the group,
omitting some visits that had formed part of our
original programme.

26th.—Arrived at Havannah Harbour, Sandwich
Island, about noon. Here a pleasant shady walk of
three miles skirting the beach led to the village and
mission station. This is one of the stations of the
Presbyterian Mission to the New Hebrides, but Mr.
McDonald, who is in charge of it, was absent from
home at the time. The houses in which the officers
of the French troops formerly stationed here resided
were pointed out to us.

We sailed once more at 5 P.M., and arrived at Dillon
Bay, Eromanga, at 9 A.M. on the following morning. The anchorage is well sheltered from the trade
winds, but quite open towards the west. A pretty
little river, well stocked with fish, flows into the
bay through a narrow winding valley between high
wooded hills. Close to the mouth of the river, under
the shelter of the hills, is the mission house where Mr.
Robertson, of the Presbyterian Mission, has been living

for the last seventeen years. The natives of Eromanga were formerly notorious as nearly the most savage and treacherous of all the New Hebrides islanders; it was here that the well-known missionary, John Williams, was murdered, and two others met the same fate shortly before Mr. Robertson came to work in the island. Now, however, a very different tale can be told, the people round the mission looked happy, contented, and well cared for; they have been trained in useful industries, for example the preparation of arrowroot, and are given a good simple education. When Mr. Robertson arrived at Eromanga in 1872, he could not go more than a mile from the mission station without imminent danger of being killed, and the native Christians voluntarily kept watch round his house for a year, to prevent an attack by the hostile people from the interior. Now both he and his wife can walk or ride all over the island without the slightest danger, and the mission work has made such progress that when Mr. Robertson takes his well-earned furlough he can leave everything in charge of the native Christian teachers, and find on his return that all has gone well.

After a short stay, which was made very pleasant by the kindness and hospitality of Mr. and Mrs. Robertson, we sailed for Noumea at 5 P.M.

On the evening of October 27th, when off Maré Island, in the Loyalty Group, Robert Heath, mate of the *Helena,* who had been gradually sinking, died, and was buried on the 29th in the cemetery at Noumea. A simple cross of wood, with name and date, was made on board by our carpenters, and placed over the grave.

We passed through the Havannah Pass about 8
A.M. on the 28th, and arrived at Noumea about 1 P.M.
Immediately after arrival, Isaac Osborn, the wounded
seaman of the *Helena*, was sent to the hospital at
Noumea, where he was well cared for and received
every attention. Coaled ship on the 29th, and sailed for
Sydney about 2 P.M., and carried the S.E. trade down
to 29° S., and light northerly winds thence to Sydney,
where we arrived about 4 P.M. on November 4th. On
arrival the Commander-in-Chief transferred his flag to
the *Orlando*.

Remained at Sydney, giving leave, coaling, and refitting, until November 21st, when we sailed for Jervis
Bay, for gun and torpedo practice.

Arrived at Jervis Bay about 7 A.M. on the 22nd.
Machine-gun practice, night-firing, and running torpedoes were carried out.

On the evening of the 23rd a most successful seining-
party was organized. About two thousand fish were
caught, including several small sharks.

A dense fog hung over the bay during the early
part of the 24th; it was partly due to a large number
of bush fires in the neighbouring country. An equally
dense fog was experienced at Sydney on the same day.
During the afternoon, however, a fresh southerly wind
cleared the fog away, and we sailed for Sydney about
5 P.M., reaching our destination early next morning
(November 25th).

During our stay in Jervis Bay some of the bolts
which secured the wooden sheathing to the hull were
found to be defective ; in consequence, instead of
accompanying the flag-ship to Hobart, we remained at

Sydney, and on December 5th went into dry dock at Cockatoo Island. Cockatoo Island, or Bilosla, is about two miles and a half from Farm Cove up the Parramatta River, and lies about midway between the entrances to Lane Cove and Ironstone Cove. It was formerly utilized as a convict prison. At the present time there is a small establishment for female prisoners, but the more important works on the island are its docks.

Close to the dock which we entered, an extremely fine new Government dock, to be named the Fitzroy dock, is being constructed, and when completed will be the finest in the southern hemisphere.

The dimensions of the new dock are as follows : Length on the blocks, 580 feet; length over all, 638 feet ; breadth of entrance, 88 feet ; depth over the sill at ordinary springs, 32 feet.

The boys from the Reformatory ship *Vernon*, which is moored close at hand, are landed on the island for recreation two or three times a week.

An odd corner near the dock had been turned into a cemetery for ship-pets, and in it were many little stones adorned with memorial verses in honour of departed favourites. Of these the following lines on a goat were probably the best :—

IN MEMORY OF BILL THE GOAT.

H.M.S. *Lizard.*

Here lays the remains of Bill the goat,
Who had no rum to oil his throat.
He joined the tetotlers for a change,
And died that night on the ship's cook's range.

Came out of dock on December 18th, and secured
to No. 2 buoy, Farm Cove.

For many months past there had been a long
drought, from which New South Wales and other
parts of Australia were suffering severely ; thousands and tens of thousands of sheep died on the runs ;
and in consequence of the continued scarcity, milk,
butter, vegetables, &c., were almost at famine prices,
although a considerable quantity was imported from
New Zealand.

The following extract from a poem written by a
South Australian, Mr. W. N. Pratt, gives some idea
of what rain means in Australia.

RAIN.

Hark to the rain ! Its cooling drops are falling
  On failing streams, on thirsty field and plain ;
Hark to the birds ! how each sweet voice is calling
  A happy blessing on the gentle rain !
And as it falls there wakes the glad refrain
From every pattering rain-drop—Hark to the rain !

Hark to the rain ! Its strange and welcome beating
  Makes music on the roof and window-pane,
And each glad heart the music keeps repeating
  Till all the notes are blended, and the strain,
From home and altar, church and holy fane,
Re-echoes up to Heaven—Hark to the rain !

Hark to the rain ! Beneath the bare earth, sleeping
  The flowers will waken at the sound again,
And swelling buds and grass come shyly peeping,
  And smile to see the long-lost, welcome rain ;
And flocks and herds, that thirsted long in vain,
Will join the joyous chorus—Hark to the rain !

*   *   *   *   *

> Hark to the rain ! as though from Heaven were falling
> God's pitying tear-drops, earthwards borne as rain ;
> But not to stay. On the dry earth they're calling—
> I've blessed you ; wake to life, and bless again.
> Bring forth your fruits, your wealth of golden grain,
> That all may eat and live—Hark to the rain !
>
> Hark to the rain ! With praise the earth is ringing,
> No voice of hers can silent now remain ;
> The fields grow green, the birds for joy are singing,
> Full flow the brooks, the flowers fresh perfume gain !
> Earth's voices call—Shall man his voice restrain ?
> No ! We with them are singing—Hark to the rain !

Greatly to the satisfaction of every one on board, we remained at Sydney over Christmas. There was plenty of time to make preparations, and from the appearance of the lower deck on Christmas Day, when the captain and visitors walked round, this time was well spent. A large quantity of green-stuff had been procured from the shore, and this, combined with various devices in coloured paper, and backed up by the well-spread tables in all the messes, presented a very bright and cherful appearance. Altogether it proved a very bright and happy Christmas.

On December 7th, at 3 P.M., we sailed for Auckland to join the squadron there, and saw the old year out during a calm and pleasant, but uneventful passage to New Zealand.

1889.

We arrived in Auckland about 3 P.M. on January 4th, and found the flag-ship in the *Calliope* dock, and the *Opal*, *Rapid*, and *Lizard* in the stream.

On the following day the mail arrived from Samoa, bringing disquieting news : there had been more fighting in the neighbourhood of Apia, in which German seamen landed from the ships had been engaged.

We remained in Auckland for rather more than a week, enjoying this opportunity of renewing the friendships formed on our last visit.

On January 12th the squadron sailed for Wellington, and arrived in Port Nicholson on the 15th, where we found the *Raven*. We had been indulging in visions of a pleasant cruise round New Zealand, and probably a sight of the beautiful Sounds, but these hopes were dashed to the ground when soon after arrival we received orders to proceed to Samoa to relieve the *Royalist*. The next few days were spent in coaling, provisioning, giving leave, and otherwise preparing for a long cruise.

On January 21st, at 11 A.M., we sailed for Samoa, the Commander-in-Chief came on board for a few minutes before we weighed, to bid the ship " *bon voyage.*" The same day the German gun-boat *Eber* arrived at

Auckland from Samoa bringing wounded men and despatches.

Picking up a strong S.E. trade about lat. 30° S., we made a quick run and arrived at Apia on February 2nd. Here we found the *Royalist*, and the German corvettes *Olga* and *Adler*. The U.S. corvette *Nipsic.* arrived the same evening, bringing mails from the *Mariposa.* The mail-steamers from San Francisco to Auckland do not call at Apia, but usually a small sailing cutter, or, as in this instance, a man-of-war, waits for the mail off Tutuila.

On February 3rd, chief engine-room artificer Richards, who had been taken ill some days earlier, was sent to the *Royalist* for passage to hospital at Auckland. We heard afterwards that he died nine days after leaving Samoa, and was buried at sea. This is the first death that has occurred among the ship's company since commissioning.

H.M.S. *Royalist* sailed for Auckland.

Lieut. Marchant, R.M.L.I., eight marines, and a signal-man, were landed for guard duties, to replace a similar guard from the *Royalist*. Their quarters were in a corrugated iron house near the beach, well in view of the ship, so that signalling was an easy matter, and less than half a mile from the British Consulate.

During our stay Captain Kane more than once entertained at dinner the British, United States, and German Consuls, and the captains of the different men-of-war, and thereby pleasanter and more cordial relations were established than had previously existed.

Although outside the harbour the sea was swarming with sharks, yet they did not seem to come inside at

all, and the men were able to bathe from the ship
whenever the weather permitted it. There was also
extremely good bathing on shore, about a quarter of
a mile from the pier, in a pretty little river, forming a
pool ten or twelve feet deep, and large enough to afford
a fair swim. More than one cricket match was played
with the European residents or the natives; the latter,
like the Tongans, are passionately fond of the game,
and seemed also inclined to take kindly to base-ball,
which was played occasionally by the Americans. In
spite of the recent fighting, everything seemed very
quiet; no fighting took place during our stay, and it
was possible to walk anywhere through the island with
perfect safety. Mataafa's camp was situated on the
rising ground about two miles from Apia; it was said
to be well fortified. Large numbers of men were to
be seen every evening coming down into Apia for
provisions ; all were armed with rifles of different sorts,
and seemed perfectly friendly. The opposing chiefs
certainly kept their men in good order ; for long no
private property of neutrals was touched by either
side, and all through the disturbance the plantations
of the different missions were entirely unharmed. The
missions in Samoa have been most successful. The
London Missionary Society and the Roman Catholic
Mission are both doing good work. The latter have their
head-quarters at Apia, where they have two churches,
and excellent schools, and as their buildings are so prominent, visitors have often imagined that the majority
of the Samoans are Roman Catholics. This however
is not the case. The total population of the Samoan
Islands is about 34,000, and of these about 23,000 are

adherents of the London Mission, about 7,000 are Roman Catholics, and the remainder are Wesleyans. The head-quarters of the London Missionary Society are at Malua, about twelve miles to the westward of Apia, where there is a flourishing training college for native teachers. The regularity with which the Samoans conduct their family prayers is very striking : every morning about six o'clock, and every evening about seven, they are to be seen in their huts singing, praying, and reading the Bible.

The small church in Apia belonging to the London Missionary Society had been given up for the use of the men wounded in the recent fighting, and was being utilized as a temporary hospital. A number of other cases were being cared for in huts near the British Consulate. All these men were attended during many weeks by the surgeons from the English and American ships in harbour.

For the first week after our arrival we had most enjoyable weather, bright and calm, but on February 10th we got our first blow. During the early morning it began to blow fresh from E. by N. and a small trading schooner, the *Matautu*, which had anchored ahead of us on the previous evening, began to drift down across our bows, and a cutter was sent to tow her clear. About 10 o'clock, as the wind increased, she again began to drag, and was thrown high and dry on to the reef. Our gunner, Mr. C. O. Martin, and a party of ten men were on board at the time rendering assistance.

As the schooner grounded on the reef, G. Munden, O.S., was washed overboard, and was with difficulty rescued by A. E. Smith, O.S., who pluckily jumped into the surf in order to carry a rope to his shipmate, and both were hauled safely on board. Fortunately, all escaped over the reef, and were taken off by boats, with no greater injury than badly cut feet from walking over coral. It continued to blow hard all day ; there was no communication with the shore. The ship was rolling heavily, all scuttles shut, and it was altogether very hot and uncomfortable. There was a slight improvement on the following day, but in consequence of the heavy swell setting into the harbour no boats left the ship. Steam was kept up constantly during this and the following gales, but so far it had not been found necessary to use the engines.

On the 12th there was a great improvement in the weather; weighed at 9 A.M., and proceeded outside for quarterly firing ; returned about 4 P.M. and moored.

The gunboat *Eber* arrived from Auckland.

On the 13th the morning was calm and fine, but heavy squalls of wind and rain came on in the afternoon.

On February 14th there was a heavy gale from N.E., with rain all day. During the morning an American three-masted schooner, the *Constitution*, half laden with stores, dragged her anchors, and ultimately struck the reef about 11 A.M., and became a total wreck. Her crew were previously taken off by boats from the *Nipsic*, and no lives were lost. During the day another small trading schooner, the *Tamasese*, was driven ashore on the beach. Towards evening the gale moderated. After each of these gales we sighted our anchors and re-moored. Although we had steam up and lower yards and top-masts down, it was never necessary to use the engines, although several of the other men-of-war were obliged to do so. This may probably be accounted for by the unusual weight of our anchors and cables; our "bowers" each weighed two hundredweight more than the *Trenton's*, a ship of a thousand tons greater burden than the *Calliope*.

During our stay at Apia, in consequence of the disturbed state of the country no leave was given to any men of a lower rating than first-class petty officer. Although this was felt as a restriction, yet the advantage of this arrangement was very evident in the good health of the ship's company, while the Americans and Germans, who were giving leave, suffered from fever and dysentery.

On the 24th the United States corvette *Vandalia* arrived to reinforce the American squadron. She was an old-fashioned wooden corvette of 2,100 tons.

During the remainder of the month and the early part of March, the weather was more settled, and there were only occasional strong winds, and a slight gale on March 7th. On March 11th the U.S.S. *Trenton*, the flag-ship of Rear-Admiral Kimberly, arrived. She was a fine old-fashioned cruiser of 4,000 tons, and was the largest ship in the harbour.

We now began to think that the worst of the season was over, and that we should be troubled with no more strong gales; but never was a greater mistake made. The following account of the hurricane which swept over the harbour is taken from the journal of one of the lieutenants:—

"On Thursday, March 14th, the barometer began to fall rapidly, but with no wind. There was, however,

G

heavy rain, and the pilots said the glass fell for that,
and that there would be no wind.   Having already
ridden out three gales no doubt added a feeling of
security.   On the 15th the glass still fell, and at 2 P.M.
reached its lowest reading, 29·11, at which time it
looked very black, rained hard, and there were light
squalls from the southward.   About 3 P.M. the wind
shifted to the north-east—we were thus just clear of the
protection of the east point of the harbour—and began
to blow fresh.   Lower yards and top-masts had been
sent down, and steam was then raised in three boilers.
By midnight it was blowing a gale, and by 4 A.M. a
hurricane; the wind was slowly shifting to the northward, thus blowing straight into the harbour.   The
driving rain and darkness made it impossible to see
if the ship dragged by bearings; but the lead and our
stern hawser, out to a kedge, told us we were gradually
getting nearer the reef.   The first accident happened
about 3 A.M., when two merchant vessels, a Danish
schooner and a German barque, collided.   The latter
sank at once, while the former weathered the storm
till much later, when she also went to pieces.   At 5
A.M. the German gun-vessel *Eber* went on the reef and
broke in pieces, going under the reef altogether, save
a small portion of her bow which reached the beach.
Four men and one officer were saved—how, they don't
know, except that they found themselves ashore.   At
daylight the *Calliope, Adler, Olga,* and *Nipsic* were all
close together and steaming hard to their anchors,
while the *Vandalia* was dragging in from outside of
them though steaming full speed.   The *Adler* collided
with her countryman, losing all her head-gear and

knocking a great hole in the *Olga's* quarter. The latter ship struck the *Nipsic*, clearing her port side and taking away her funnel. About 7.30 A.M., the *Nipsic*, not being able to keep steam without a funnel, ran on shore, and was expected to break up; she, however, did not do so, being fortunately on a soft patch. Her bowsprit was right over the road along the beach, and over it her crew, save six, got ashore. The *Adler*, which had been dragging closer to the reef all the morning, touched about 8 A.M.; at the same moment the cables were slipped, and she was thrown bodily on top of the coral on her beam ends, keel to seaward, decks vertical. Seeing she was a ship of about 900 tons, and under ordinary circumstances the reef is never more than two feet covered, this gives a good idea of the sea then running. Her crew were of course thrown into the water, but most of them managed to get back under the lee of the ship, and had to remain there till 10 A.M. next day. By this time the *Vandalia* was close to the *Calliope*, whilst the latter had sensibly closed the *Olga*. The *Calliope* and *Olga* collided while the latter was steaming ahead, carrying away the remains of her head-gear and badly wounding the *Calliope's* fore-yard, carrying away its lashing, and leaving it swinging about and no easy matter to secure. The *Calliope* and *Vandalia* collided twice, the former first losing her jibboom, and secondly all the securings of her bowsprit, while the latter was damaged in hull. Steam had been raised in a fourth boiler about 4 A.M., and after that in all six boilers; but as the ship was steaming ahead nearly all the time, it was long before a full head of steam was ready. The port cable had parted about 7 A.M., the sheet cable was slipped about 8 A.M., and finally about 9.30 A.M., full steam being ready, the starboard cable was slipped and the ship started to sea steaming full speed. For some time, which seemed an age, the ship remained stationary, then slowly gathering way she cleared the *Vandalia* and passed close to the *Trenton*. The latter had dragged, and was now, with rudder and post gone, screw off, and water streaming in through her hawse-pipes, lying fair in the middle of the narrowest part of the passage. The water was breaking about a hundred yards off the reef, so its extremity was not to be seen ; thus leaving a narrow margin in which to turn up and clear the *Trenton*. For some seconds it seemed as if we could not possibly clear her without running on to the reef, but by magnificent management of the helm we just cleared her stern, our fore-yard passing over her poop as we rolled to leeward. The *Trenton's* crew, headed by Admiral Kimberly, gave us three hearty cheers as we passed, which our men as heartily returned. One minute after we passed the *Trenton* she was lost to sight in the driving spray and rain. Before leaving the harbour, the cutter, dingy, skiff, and copper-punt had been washed away, and at the entrance of the harbour the jolly-boat went from astern. After passing the *Trenton* the way was clear, and we got out, making about a knot and a half at the outside, although the engines were developing sufficient power to drive her fourteen knots in smooth water. Once at sea, it became a struggle between the engines and the wind and sea. Fortunately everything worked well, and we gradually cleared the land, steering to the northward.

" After our departure the *Vandalia* dragged in and struck close to where the *Nipsic* was on shore, sinking to her upper deck. The greater part of the crew took to the masts : some tried to get across the short distance which separated them from the *Nipsic,* but owing to the tremendous sea and strong current were swept away and drowned ; none who tried it reached the shore. The *Trenton* dragged in, and about 5 P.M. fouled the *Olga,* clearing her port side and shifting her after bulk-head. To avoid further damage the latter slipped and ran ashore on a sandy beach. She was little damaged below the water-line, and made no water. The *Trenton* dragged on, and finally struck and sank close to the *Vandalia,* filling to her main deck. Being to windward of the *Vandalia* she sheltered her and saved the crew, many of whom were almost incapacitated by exposure."

The following graphic description of the disaster, taken from the *Army and Navy Journal,* New York, gives a good idea of what took place in the harbour of Apia during that eventful day :—

" A few days preceding the hurricane the weather was cloudy, and the barometer had been steadily falling, but no one anticipated the storm which began to set in on Friday afternoon, March 15th. By 11 o'clock at night the wind had increased to a gale, and the rain began to fall at midnight. The pitching of the vessels was fearful. Every man was kept at work. The *Eber* began to drag her anchors at midnight, and an hour later the *Vandalia's* were also dragging. However, by using full steam power, they both succeeded in keeping well off the reef and away from the other vessels. By 3 o'clock the situation had become alarming. Nearly

every vessel in the harbour was dragging its anchor, and
there was imminent danger of a collision. The little
gunboat *Eber* was the first to go ashore. Suddenly she
shot forward as if making a last struggle to escape destruction. The current, however, bore her off to the
right, and her prow struck the port quarter of the *Nipsic*,
carrying away several feet of the *Nipsic's* rail and one
boat. The *Eber* then fouled the *Olga*, swung around
broadside to the wind, was lifted high on the crest of a
great wave, and carried broadside on the reef. She
struck fairly, rolled over towards the open sea, and disappeared from view.

" Presently a man was seen clinging to a small wharf
near by. Willing hands grasped him and pulled him
upon the shore. He proved to be Lieutenant Gaedeke,
the only officer of the *Eber* saved. Four sailors from the
Eber were seen struggling in the water near shore at
about the same time. They were rescued by natives.
It was about 6 in the morning when the *Eber*
foundered.

" Half-an-hour later the *Adler* was seen going on to
the reef broadside on, about 200 yards from where the
Eber struck. She was lifted on top of the reef, and
turned completely over on her side. Nearly her entire
hull was out of water; her deck was at right angles
with the water and facing the shore; consequently that
portion of the vessel was well protected from the storm.
Most of her men were struggling in the water, but had
only a few feet to swim to reach the deck, where they
clung in safety. Of the 130 officers and men aboard,
twenty men were drowned or killed when the steamer
capsized. All of the officers, including Captain Fritze,

who was in command of the German squadron, were saved.

" It was only by the most skilful management that the *Nipsic* was saved from the same fate. She narrowly escaped destruction by being run into by the *Olga*, and it was the blow which she received from that vessel that finally sent her ashore. The *Nipsic* had on full steam, and in trying to avoid the German ran down and sunk the schooner *Lily*. The *Nipsic* got well away from the reef after she struck the *Lily*, and her men had attached a hawser to a heavy eight-inch rifle on the forward deck, and were preparing to hoist the gun overboard to assist her anchors when the *Olga* again struck her amidships ; her bowsprit passed over the port side, and, after carrying away a boat and splintering the rail, struck the smoke-stack fairly in the centre, and it fell to the deck. Having lost her smoke-stack, the *Nipsic* was unable to keep her steam power up. Captain Mullan saw that any further attempt to save his vessel would be useless, so her head was turned to the shore, and she ran a straight course of 100 yards to the sandy beach in front of the American Consulate. Orders were given to lower the boats, but the falls of the first did not work properly, and the men were thrown into the water and drowned. The other, containing E. Z. Derr, the ship's surgeon, and half-a-dozen sick men, was lowered in safety, but it capsized before it reached the shore. The men half swam, half floated, until they came within reach of the natives, who were standing waist-deep in the surf, when they were pulled out on the beach. Several men on the *Nipsic* ran to the rail and jumped overboard, among them being Lieutenant

R. G. Davenport. They reached the shore in safety,
except two sailors. By this time, every man aboard
had crowded on the forecastle. The natives shouted to
those on deck to throw a line. Double hawsers were
made fast from deck to shore, and the natives gathered round the lines to assist the men off. Sepmann
Taea, chief of the Apia district, and Salu Ana, King
Mataafa's secretary, directed the men in their work.

"The scene was one of intense excitement. Above
the roar of the wind and waves could be heard the
voices of the officers shouting to the men on deck,
mingled with the cries and singing of the Samoans as
they stood battling against the surf, risking their lives
to save the sailors. The American and English residents of Apia were also on the spot willing to render
assistance. Captain Mullan and several other officers
stood by the rail where the hawsers were made fast, and
directed the movements of the men. All who were in
any way sick or injured were allowed to leave first.
The seas were rolling so high under the bows of the
steamer that when the men had advanced ten feet down
the ropes, they would often be entirely submerged, and
nothing but the efforts of the natives prevented them
from being washed off and carried away. Captain
Mullan finally found himself on deck with Lieutenant
John A. Shearman. The captain, being unable to swim,
did not care to trust to descending the rope by means
of his hands and legs, so he procured an empty water-
cask, which he attached to the hawser. When he was
seated in the cask, Shearman stood alone on the deck
and started his commander down the ropes. The
lieutenant then climbed down the rope in the usual

way, and the *Nipsic* was left alone to battle with the waves.

" Next followed a collision between the *Calliope* and *Vandalia*. The jibboom of the *Calliope* was carried away and the heavy timbers of the *Vandalia* shivered, every man who stood upon the poop being thrown from his feet. A hole had been torn below the rail and the water rushed into the cabin. Lieutenant J. W. Carlin, executive officer, was practically in charge of the vessel, as Captain Schoonmaker had been thrown across the cabin the night before and severely injured. His head had been badly cut and one ear almost torn away. Notwithstanding his injuries, he faced the storm, and stood by the side of his first officer until the sea finally swept him off to his death. He was in such a dazed and weakened condition, however, that he was able to do but little towards directing the movements of the ship. Of all the officers who stood by their posts and did their duty nobly in the face of danger, none have received more commendation than Lieutenant Carlin, who had been on duty since the morning before, and had not tasted food in all that time. Though weak and exhausted, he kept his position by the side of Captain Schoonmaker and Lieutenant J. C. Wilson, the navigating officer, and encouraged every one around him. It was finally determined that the only course left was to beach the ship. Two of her anchor chains were slipped, and a full head of steam put on. The *Vandalia* was a quarter of a mile from the *Nipsic*, and she was obliged to run along the edge of the reef the whole distance in order to reach the sandy beach beyond. She came on until her bow struck in the soft sand, about a

hundred yards off the shore, and swung around broadside to the beach. It was nearly 11 o'clock when the
ship struck, and notwithstanding her easy position, it
soon became apparent that her officers and crew were
in great danger. The vessel was filling with water and
settling down. Lying as she did almost broadside to
the wind, the seas broke over her furiously, and poured
down her hatches. By noon the whole of her gun-deck
was under water, and from that time on the condition
of the men was the most pitiable that could be
imagined. Torrents of water swept over the rails and
knocked them from their feet. Most sought refuge in
the rigging. A few officers only remained upon the
poop. Three natives were found who were willing to
venture out in the surf with a cord and attempt to reach
the vessel. The men entered the water a quarter of a
mile above the spot where the steamer lay, and struggled
bravely to reach the ship ; but, expert swimmers as
they were, they were unable to overcome the force of
the current.

" The first man who came ashore was Chief Engineer
A. S. Greene. He was swept from the poop three times.
Twice he succeeded in catching a rope as he fell, and
drew himself back on to the steamer. The third
time he was unable to reach her again. He then swam
to the side of the *Nipsic* and caught hold of a rope, and
tried in vain to draw himself up. Finding his strength
failing, he let go of the rope and drifted back near the
bow of the *Vandalia*, caught a piece of floating wreckage,
and clung to it with all the strength he had left. The
natives saw his head above the water, and they clasped
each other's hands, formed a long line stretching out

into the current, and the native furthest out clutched him by his arms and brought him ashore. Captain Schoonmaker was still clinging to the rail on the poop of the *Vandalia*, Carlin doing his best to hold the captain on. Every one saw the captain could not stand against the rush of the water much longer, and he remarked to those about him that he would have to go soon. An attempt was made to get him up in the rigging, but he was too weak to climb. At last a great wave struck the *Vandalia* on her port quarter; a machine-gun was washed from its fastenings and sent whirling across the deck, striking the captain on the head; and either killing him outright or knocking him insensible, the wave swept him off the deck; he sank without a struggle, and was seen no more.

"Paymaster Arms and Pay Clerk Roach were lying upon the deck exhausted, but clinging with all the strength they possessed to anything which came within their grasp. They were swept off together. Arms sank in a moment. Roach drifted over to the stem of the *Nipsic*, where he grasped a rope. He was a large, fleshy man, and, being greatly exhausted, could not possibly draw himself up. His hold upon the rope was soon broken, and he finally sank under the vessel. Lieutenant Sutton, a marine officer of the *Vandalia*, died in much the same way. Weakened by long exposure and the terrible strain to which he was subjected, he was unable to retain his hold longer, and was finally washed overboard and drowned. Lieutenant Carlin, the last man to leave the deck, climbed into the mizen-top, where he sank utterly exhausted. His legs hung down through the opening to the platform, and a sailor, who was sitting underneath, appreciating the noble work of his officer, took the lieutenant's legs in his hands, and rubbed them until the blood circulated freely. More than one man who was clinging to the ratlines gave way under the terrible strain and fell to the deck, only to be washed over the side of the ship and drowned.

" The stem of the *Nipsic* had by this time swung out straight from the shore, so that the distance between the vessels was not more than twenty yards. A white man named Vickering, who had been watching the scene from the shore, went aboard the *Nipsic* and threw a line to the *Vandalia*. A sailor caught it, and a small rope was made fast from the foremast of the *Vandalia* to the stem of the *Nipsic*. A few men escaped in that way, but before all could be taken off the line parted. The *Nipsic's* stem then swung back to the shore, and it was impossible to get another line across. This was the only connection the *Vandalia* had with the shore during the whole day. About 4 o'clock in the afternoon the *Trenton* was seen coming down upon the *Olga*, and a collision seemed inevitable. The condition of the flagship was pitiable. At 10 o'clock in the morning her rudder and propeller had been carried away by a piece of wreckage. The hawse-pipes were, unfortunately, on the berth-deck, instead of on the gun-deck. Ever since the *Trenton* was built, this has been regarded as a piece of faulty construction, as the openings were so low down that, with a heavy sea rolling, it was almost impossible to keep the water out of the vessel. Efforts were made to close the pipes, but the coverings were blown off, the water rushed in on the berth-decks, found its way to the hatches, and poured down into the fire-room and extinguished the fires. From 10 o'clock in the morning until 6 in the evening, when she grounded, the *Trenton* held out against the storm without steam or rudder. Admiral Kimberly, Captain Farquhar, and Lieutenant Brown stood upon the bridge the whole day and directed the movement of the ship. As soon as the steam gave out the mizen storm-sail was set. Oil was also poured overboard, but it had no effect.

"The *Trenton* succeeded in keeping clear of the reef until the middle of the afternoon, when she came broadside on toward the reef. Then every man was ordered into the port rigging, so that a compact mass of humanity could be used as sails, and at the same time kept the weight of the vessel on the side next to the storm. This novel expedient saved the *Trenton* from destruction. The wind struck against the men in the rigging, and forced the vessel out into the bay again. Suddenly the Stars and Stripes were seen flying from the gaff of the *Trenton*. Previous to this no vessel in the harbour had raised a flag, as the storm was raging so furiously at sunrise that that ceremony was neglected. It seemed now as if those in the ship knew she was doomed, and had determined to go down with the flag of their country floating. The stern of the *Trenton* was nearing the *Olga's* bows, and Captain Von Erhardt, believing that destruction was upon him, slipped his anchors, and attempted to steam away. He was too late, however, for just as the *Olga* commenced to move, her bow came into contact with the starboard quarter of the flag-ship; the *Olga's* bowsprit and figure-head were carried away, the timbers on the *Trenton's* quarter shivered, several boats dropped from their davits, and the American flag which had floated from the *Trenton* was carried away, and fell to the deck of the *Olga*. Fortunately the vessels drifted apart after the collision, and the *Olga* was run aground in the soft mud in the softest part of the bay, and no lives were lost.

"It was now after 5 o'clock, and the light was beginning to fade away. In half-an-hour the *Trenton* had drifted on to within a few yards of the *Vandalia's* bow, and the men who were in the rigging of the latter vessel trembled with fear as they saw the *Trenton* approach. Suddenly a shout was borne across the waters. The sound of 450 voices broke upon the air, and was heard above the roar of the tempest. 'Three cheers for the *Vandalia!*' was the cry that warmed the hearts of the dying men in the rigging. The shout died away upon the storm, and there arose from the quivering masts of the sunken ship a response so feeble that it was scarcely heard upon shore. The men, who felt they were looking death in the face, aroused themselves to the effort, and united in a faint cheer for the flag-ship. Those who were standing on shore listened in silence, for that feeble cry was the saddest they had ever heard. Every heart was melted to pity. 'God help them!' was passed from one man to another. The sound of music next came across the water. The *Trenton's* band was playing *The Star-Spangled Banner*. The thousand men on sea and shore had never before heard strains of music at such a time as this. The collision of the *Trenton* and *Vandalia*, which every one thought would crush the latter vessel to pieces, proved to be the salvation of the men in the rigging. Notwithstanding the tremendous force of the waves, the *Trenton* dragged back slowly, and when her stem finally struck the side of the *Vandalia*, there was no shock, and she gradually swung around broadside to the sunken ship. As soon as the vessels touched, the men in the mizen rigging crawled out on the yards and jumped to the deck of the *Trenton.* The men escaped just in time, for, as the last one left, the mizen-mast of the *Vandalia* fell. The mainmast of the *Vandalia* fell soon after. The men who escaped to the deck of the *Trenton* had clung to the *Vandalia's* rigging nearly twelve hours. All were weak and exhausted, and many had received severe injuries.

" The *Calliope* had succeeded by the aid of her powerful engines in holding on until about 10 o'clock. The *Olga* had several times collided with her, and carried away her fore-yard, crushed nearly all her boats, and snapped one of her cables. She gradually drifted down on the inner reef, and was holding on by a single anchor. The *Trenton* and the *Olga* were dragging down upon and threatening to foul her, when Captain Kane took the desperate resolve which eventually saved his vessel. Forcing his fires until the boilers were under a tremendous pressure of steam, he paid out on his single cable, so as to be able to clear the *Olga's* stern. Suddenly, when his stern was within twenty feet of the reef, he slipped his chain from the locker, and the next moment the *Calliope* drew forward into the very teeth of the gale, her propeller making eighty-five revolutions per minute. Clearing the *Olga*, she steamed by within speaking distance of the *Trenton*, passing between that vessel and the western reef. And then from those

400 men standing face to face with death broke forth
a ringing Yankee cheer to speed the plucky English-
man on his way, and as the *Calliope* disappeared in the
mist and driving rain an answering shout came back
upon the gale."

March 17*th.*—All Saturday the storm continued without sensibly moderating. In spite of the way the ship was
knocking about, accidents were very rare ; the only man
seriously injured was Thomas John, carpenter's mate,
who was washed against the coaming of a hatchway by a
heavy sea, just before the ship left the harbour, and had
one side of his face stove in.

There were some heavy squalls during the middle
watch on Sunday morning, but towards noon the wind
and sea moderated slightly, and things were gradually
got into something like order ; and at 5.30 P.M. we were
able to go to evening quarters, and have short " stand-
up " prayers, with special thanksgiving and Collect from
the " Form of Prayers to be used at Sea."

The speed was reduced about 4 A.M. on Sunday morning, and we continued steaming slowly to the northward
until 8 A.M. on Monday, the 18th, when the storm being
now fairly over, we altered our course and headed once
more for Apia.

We sighted Apia about 5 P.M., but did not arrive off
the harbour until dusk, when it was considered advisable
to stand off for the night. Every one was on deck
eagerly looking out to see what ships remained afloat.

From the state of things when we left, the very worst
was to be feared, and now we did not gain very much
information; the outer part of the harbour was absolute-
ly cleared, only some masts were to be seen above the

trees on Matautu Point, which shut out the inner part of the harbour from view.

About 8 A.M. on the 19th we arrived once more at the entrance to the harbour, fired a gun and hoisted the signal for a pilot, as no one could tell what obstructions there might now be in the harbour.

As soon as we got inside we were able to see the extent of the disaster. The harbour indeed presented a strange and melancholy sight. The three American ships, *Trenton, Vandalia,* and *Nipsic* were close companions in misfortune. The *Vandalia* was sunk to her upper deck, a perfect wreck, only her foremast standing, the *Trenton* sunk in shallow water; but being a large ship, all her gun ports were still above water; her masts were still standing and colours flying. The *Nipsic* was lodged well up on a sandy beach about eighty yards to the eastward, and still further in the same direction was the *Olga,* with her bowsprit and figure-head smashed, and a large hole in her quarter. The *Adler* was a strange sight, lying high and dry on the reef on her beam ends, her keel turned to seawards; although her deck was vertical, and the strain when striking the reef must have been tremendous, all her guns remained lashed in their places.

On shore there were abundant traces of the power of the wind. The road running parallel to the beach was covered with sand and wreckage, trees had been blown down, and a wooden bridge over the river swept away. The houses had suffered to a less extent than might have been expected.

We had now only one anchor to trust to, and in the unsettled state of the weather Captain Kane decided to leave Apia as soon as possible.

H

Coaling began almost immediately, and, as we were short of boats the *Trenton* kindly lent her cutter, and the *Olga* her steam pinnace to assist to expedite matters. During the day three of the London Missionary Society's missionaries and other residents came off to the ship to offer their congratulations on our escape. By Wednesday night 150 tons of coal had been got on board, and everything was made ready for sailing. The *Trenton* kindly gave us one of her cutters to take the place of the boat we had lost.

On Thursday, March 21st, at 6.30 A.M., Lieutenant Emsmann of the *Olga* came on board for passage to Sydney, and at 7.15 we weighed anchor, saluted Admiral Kimberly with thirteen guns, and proceeded to sea, bound for Sydney. All on board were heartily glad to see the last of Apia. As we left the harbour it was observed that the efforts which had been made to float the *Nipsic* had proved successful, and she was once more afloat. We heard afterwards that after an unsuccessful attempt to reach Auckland she returned to Samoa, and subsequently made her way to Honolulu under sail.

On our way round the eastern end of Upolu we overtook the small schooner which had been despatched the day before with mails to meet the San Francisco steamer off Tutuila. She had been ashore in Apia harbour during the hurricane, and had lost the greater part of her keel, and was now ineffectually trying to beat against a head wind. We took her in tow for about fifty miles, and dropped her off Tutuila, in plenty of time to catch the mail.

After a calm and uneventful passage we arrived at Sydney on April 4th, and were very pleased to find

ourselves once more swinging round a buoy in Farm
Cove. We were fairly astonished at the enthusiasm
which our recent experiences had aroused, and by the
warmth of the reception which we received.

As we passed South Head, the Permanent Artillery
turned out, and gave three hearty cheers, and as we
slowly steamed up the harbour we met a like kindly
recognition from the passengers in the numerous ferry
steamers and pleasure boats. We were of course very
quickly boarded by a crowd of reporters, but even the
energetic representatives of the press were forestalled by
Lord Carrington, who was waiting for the ship in his
steam launch, and boarding her before she reached the
buoy, congratulated the captain most heartily on the
escape of the *Calliope*.

For the next two or three days the friends of officers and men came off in great numbers to offer their
congratulations and get a look at the ship, and letters
and telegrams came from friends in Melbourne and other
places which we had visited.

The *Egeria* was the only man-of-war in harbour when
we arrived ; but on April 11th, the *Opal* arrived from
Auckland, and the *Swinger* from Hobart; and on the
following day the *Royalist* arrived from Auckland.

On April 13th the *Olga* arrived from Samoa, in company with the mail-steamer *Lubeck ;* she first made fast
to the flag-ship's buoy, and later in the day went up to
Mort's Dock, where she underwent a thorough refit, and
subsequently returned to Germany not much the worse
for her rough experiences at Samoa.

Shortly after our arival in Sydney, Thomas John was
sent to St. Vincent's Hospital, and after some months,

in consequence of the serious nature of his injuries, was
sent to England and invalided out of the service.

On April 15th the *Orlando, Lizard,* and *Raven* arrived
from New Zealand. As soon as she was made fast to
No. 1 buoy, " Hands cheer ship " was piped on board
the flag-ship, and three cheers for the *Calliope* were
given with thorough good-will.

On April 25th Lady Carrington very kindly gave a
picnic to the ship's company. Of course it was impossible for all to go, but about 180 seamen and marines
accepted the invitation, and spent a most enjoyable day
at the National Park. Those who were obliged to remain
on board were not forgotten, as a good knife or pipe was
sent to each.

A month in Farm Cove afforded opportunities for
excursions to the Blue Mountains and other places.
The most interesting natural objects in the neighbourhood are undoubtedly the Jenolan Caves, which are
situated about twenty-seven miles from Katoomba. These
caves are said to be the finest in the world. Their
name is derived from that of a surveyor, J. E. Nolan.

During the first week in May, Sydney was full of
clergy from all parts of the colonies who were attending
the Church Congress, where many interesting subjects
were being discussed under the presidency of Bishop
Barry. Immediately after the congress, Bishop Barry
left for England, having resigned the bishopric of
Sydney.

On May 1st a fine new railway bridge over the
Hawkesbury River was formally opened. The captain
and officers were invited to attend the ceremony.

This bridge was built by the Union Bridge Company

of New York ; it has seven spans, each 416 feet in length, and its foundations are 162 feet deep.

On May 10th, at 4 P.M., we sailed for Adelaide in company with the *Orlando*. After a pleasant passage we arrived at Largs Bay, in the Gulf of St. Vincent, about 5 A.M. on May 15th. At present there is no sheltered harbour near Adelaide, and large vessels lie at the Semaphore anchorage in Largs Bay. Here the mail-steamers embark and discharge their mails, which are conveyed to Melbourne and Sydney by rail. We anchored about two miles from the shore, about equally distant from the Semaphore and Largs Bay piers, from both of which there is railway communication with Port Adelaide and Adelaide. Port Adelaide is the principal seaport in South Australia : it is a small town of three or four thousand inhabitants, and has considerable trade, which is now chiefly carried on by means of the mail-steamers, though formerly small vessels took a larger share, and gave the port a more lively appearance.

Adelaide, the capital of South Australia, is situated on the River Torrens, about six miles from the Gulf of St. Vincent ; it is connected with Port Adelaide by road and rail. The city was founded in 1837 by Colonel Light; it is divided by the river into North and South Adelaide. Including streets and reserves the total area of the city is five square miles ; it is well laid out with broad straight streets, and a fine central square. The principal street, King William Street, is two chains in width. Tramways traverse the main thoroughfares, and extend as far as the suburbs. The public buildings, the Town Hall, the Post Office, and several banks and offices, are good specimens of architecture. The Botanical Gardens are exceedingly good; they cover an area of forty acres, and are supplemented by a park of over eighty acres, in which there is a good Zoological Garden.

The population of Adelaide exclusive of suburbs is over 40,000, and including suburbs is not far short of 120,000. Like most other colonial towns it has a good public library, museum, and picture gallery; the latter, though at present a small collection, contains some exceedingly good pictures. There is a flourishing University, which occupies some fine buildings of considerable architectural merit. The plain on which the city stands is walled in on its eastern and southern sides by the Mount Lofty range of mountains, which form a beautiful background to the landscape.

Our short stay in South Australian waters was a very gay time. There was a reception and ball at Government House; picnics, dinners, and dances were given by different residents, and a very successful *conversazione* was held at the University; the fine buildings were well filled by a crowd of guests; selections of music, scientific experiments, and short lectures on interesting scientific subjects occupied the evening very pleasantly.

A shooting party went for a couple of days to Strathalbyn, a small township about forty miles from Adelaide by rail. The railway passes over the Mount Lofty Range, and through very pretty fertile country, hilly and wooded. In consequence of the recent rains the country was looking its best—grass fresh and green, and sheep and cattle in good condition. Duck, quail, plover, and hares were obtained in tolerable abundance ; there are also wild turkeys to be had in the neighbourhood, but none were met with on this occasion.

A football team from the ships met and defeated a Rugby Union team from Adelaide and the neighbourhood.

The first few days of our stay were fine and bright, but later strong winds and rain-squalls prevailed.

Steamers plied between the Semaphore pier and the ships, but owing to the heavy swell even these were often an uncomfortable means of getting ashore.

After a most enjoyable stay we sailed for Melbourne at midnight on May 25th. We met a strong headwind and sea, and did not arrive off the entrance to Port Phillip until 2.30 P.M. on the 28th, and anchored in Hobson's Bay about 7 P.M., having been slightly delayed by fog. The Exhibition had been closed for some months, but there was still much to see in Melbourne and the neighbourhood. An exceedingly good cyclorama of the Battle of Waterloo was attracting large numbers of people, and was well worth a visit. Rather a long day suffices for a visit to Ballarat, the second city of Victoria. It is ninety-six miles from Melbourne ; at present there is no direct line, and a long detour through Geelong makes a journey of four hours necessary. The town of Ballarat owes its importance to gold-mining ; it lies in the midst of an extensive district which has been without parallel as a gold-producing region. The town at present contains about 40,000 inhabitants ; the streets are broad and straight. The principal thoroughfare,

Doveton Street, is of unusual width; it has a fine
avenue of trees down the centre, with a roadway on
each side sufficient to admit a tram-line in addition
to ordinary traffic.   On the outskirts of the town is
a small lake, much resorted to by the lovers of sailing
and rowing.   Not far off are some pretty botanical
gardens, which contain a beautiful fernery, and some
very fine pieces of sculpture.   In the town there is
a small art gallery, but as yet it contains few
pictures of any merit.

On May 31st a team from the *Orlando* and *Calliope*
played the Maori football team, which had recently
visited England.   The naval team was, of course, easily
defeated by their formidable opponents; but the game
was a pleasant one throughout, and attracted a large
number of spectators.

June 2nd.—The *Orlando* and *Calliope* sailed at 8 A.M.,
and proceeded independently to Jervis Bay. We passed
the Heads about 3.30 P.M.   There was a strongly
marked tide-rip at the entrance; the tide was setting in
very strongly, apparently at about the rate of six knots.

We arrived in Jervis Bay about 10 A.M. on June 5th,
and found the flag-ship occupied with prize-firing. This
and the two following days were employed running
torpedoes, prize-firing, &c.

Sailed for Sydney at 6.30 P.M. on the 8th, and arrived
in Farm Cove about 9 A.M. the following day.   As
soon as possible after our arrival, William Rolfe, cox-
swain of the steam pinnace, who had received serious
injuries from a fall during our stay in Largs Bay, was
sent to St. Vincent's Hospital.   He died on the following morning, and was buried in the naval section of

Rookwood Cemetery on June 11th. The *Orlando's* band accompanied the funeral procession from the hospital to Redfern Station, and played exceedingly well.

At 8 P.M. on June 14th the *Calliope* went into dock at Cockatoo Island, for examination of her sheathing. A report of her condition was afterwards forwarded to the Admiralty.

June 25th.—A party of seamen and marines attended the laying of the foundation-stone of the new Sailors' Home in Charlotte Place. Mrs. Fairfax was unable to attend on account of illness, and Lady Carrington performed the ceremony in her place. The new building will afford much better accommodation than the present house, and is in a more central position. On the evening of June 28th the ship came out of dock, and lashed alongside the wharf for the night. On the following morning returned to Farm Cove. On the same day the *Orlando* sailed for Norfolk Island, and to look out for H.M.S. *Dart*, about whose safety some anxiety was felt, as one of her boats had been picked up on the north coast of New Zealand.

On the afternoon of the 30th the *Dart* arrived after a stormy passage of twenty-five days from Auckland. She had experienced very heavy gales off the North Cape, when she lost the boat which was afterwards picked up; and again when getting near the Australian coast she fell in with more heavy weather and lay-to for seven days. Two of her crew were washed overboard during these gales, but were both saved.

On July 5th a large afternoon dance was given by the captain and officers. The ship was prettily decorated with flags and flowers, and looked very well. Large quantities of beautiful flowers had been kindly sent by friends on shore. About 350 people accepted the invitation, and dancing was carried on vigorously on the quarter-deck and poop.

During June and July of this year Santley was making a tour of the chief Australian cities. His concerts at Sydney and Melbourne were most enjoyable.

We sailed for Noumea about 1 P.M. on July 9th; met with fair winds, and made a sailing passage of it for a great part of the way. Arrived at Noumea on July 16th shortly before noon. H.M.S. *Lizard* had arrived some hours earlier.

July 16th.—Saluted French flag with twenty-one guns. The French men-of-war *Thétis* and *Saône* were in harbour when we arrived.

There was great indignation amongst the French residents generally, which was expressed more forcibly than politely in the local papers, because the two English ships had arrived just too late for the centenary of the storming of the Bastille in 1789. There had been great festivities, including a ball at Government House, races, regatta, &c.; everything, however, was over, excepting a dance in the town hall, which took place on the evening of the 16th.

On July 23rd there was a reception at Government House at 8.30 P.M. Madame Pardon, the wife of the Governor, was the only lady present. Talking and smoking were the only amusements.

On July 26th the captain gave a small afternoon dance on board. About twenty-five of the principal residents, including the Governor and Madame Pardon, came, and seemed to thoroughly enjoy their novel surroundings.

On July 27th, at 9 A.M., weighed, and started on a cruise round the New Hebrides.

We reached Aneityum, the southernmost island of the group, on July 29th, and anchored for a few hours in Port Inyung, or Anelcauhaut Harbour. The island is mountainous and wooded; the highest point is about 2,800 feet above the sea. On the slopes of the hills there is a large quantity of fine timber, especially kauri pine, which is cut up at saw-mills about half a mile from the beach, and exported to Sydney. There was heavy rain during the day, and walking through the thick brushwood or over roughly-made paths was dirty work. There is a village and mission station close to the beach, but Mr. Laurie, the missionary, was absent from home at the time of our visit. At 4 P.M. weighed and proceeded.

Sighted the volcano in Tanua about 1 A.M. on July 30th, and about 9 A.M. were off Weasisi mission station; here also the missionary was absent at the annual meeting, and everything being reported quiet, we proceeded for Eromanga, and arrived in Dillon Bay about 9 A.M. on the 31st, where we anchored in fourteen fathoms. Mr. Robertson, who had entertained us so hospitably on our former visit, was now absent on a year's furlough in New South Wales, where he was occupied with seeing translations of the Gospels through the press, and in stirring up an interest in missionary work throughout the colony. Everything, however, seemed to be going on well—the natives looked happy and prosperous, and the native teacher, who had been left in charge, reported

all well, and seemed pleased to hear that we had seen
Mr. Robertson at Sydney. We sailed at 5 P.M., and
arrived at Havannah Harbour, in Sandwich Island or
Efate, about noon on the following day. Here also
everything was reported quiet, and after a short stay we
proceeded once more. About 8 A.M. on August 2nd
arrived at the Foreland anchorage, Api (or Epi) Island ;
lowered a boat and communicated with the shore, but
all being well we proceeded at once for Mallicolo, or as
it is also written, Malekula.

August 2nd.—Arrived at Port Sandwich about 2 P.M.,
and anchored in the sheltered harbour close to the shore.
The French corvette *Saône* arrived later in the day.

Weighed at 7 A.M. on August 3rd, and steamed along
the eastern side of Malekula. About 11 A.M. arrived
off Oulua ; our surgeon went ashore to attend a sick
child at the " Amy Gertrude Russell " mission station.
After a delay of a couple of hours we proceeded along
the coast to Port Stanley, which we reached about
5 P.M.

We entered the harbour through a narrow channel
between two of the islands which shelter the anchorage.
The scene was a striking one : on our starboard side was
the island of Urombo, a small but densely-wooded and
thickly-populated island, edged with a brilliant line of
white beach, glistening in the sunshine, and broken here
and there by groups of native boats. As we steamed
slowly past, two missionaries, surrounded by a crowd of
natives, came down on the beach to watch the ship. On
our port hand was another low island, with its belt
of glittering sand forming a strong contrast to the
dark green of the dense vegetation behind. In the

harbour we found the mission ship *Dayspring*. The New Hebrides Mission have stations in Aneityum, Tanua, Eromanga, Efate, Epi, Malekula, Malo, and Espiritu Santo, which are supported by the Presbyterian churches in Scotland, Canada, Australia, and New Zealand. Their mission ship *Dayspring* has the important duties to perform of bringing stores to the different islands, and conveying the missionaries to and from their stations. The object of the *Dayspring's* visit to Port Stanley was to establish a new mission station on Urombo. There were in all four missionaries on board—Mr. Fraser of Epi, Mr. Morton of Pangkinnu, Malekula, Mr. Landels of Malo, and Mr. Gillan, who was to start work on Urombo; the three former were assisting to build the house and give the new-comer a fair start.

On Sunday, August 4th, Captain Braithwaite, of the *Dayspring*, accompanied by Mr. and Mrs. Fraser, Mr. and Mrs. Landels, Mr. and Mrs. Gillan, and Mr. Morton, with several native Christians, came on board to church. The natives sat very gravely with books in their hands all through the service, but although they knew a little English, it is not likely that they understood very much of what was going on.

At 6 A.M. on the 5th we weighed and proceeded eight miles up the coast to two small islands, Rana and Wala, in order to inquire into some recent aggressions on the part of the natives. Mr. Morton and Mr. Gillan accompanied us to assist in the inquiry. Numbers of native canoes with picturesque sails and wild-looking crews were moving about in all directions. Both islands were thickly wooded, and appeared to have large numbers of

inhabitants.   We returned to Urombo about 3 P.M.,
disembarked our passengers, and took on board again two
of our carpenters who had been sent on shore to assist
in the house-building, and sailed immediately for Santo,

6th.—Arrived at Tongoa, a small island at the
southern extremity of Espiritu Santo about 7 A.M. The
harbour was very pretty—a beautifully-sheltered anchorage shut in by richly-wooded islands.   The mission
station was on the small island of Tongoa, and   seemed
in a very flourishing condition.

Mr. and Mrs. Armand have only been at Tongoa two
years, but in that time very much has been done.   The
house and garden are beautifully neat and well kept. A
broad clearing has been made through the trees, stretching from the mission house to the sea on both sides.
and important work has been carried on with the
natives.   The native huts are very poor affairs, scarcely
more than a thatched roof resting on the ground, and
no walls worth speaking of.   Bows and arrows, clubs,
and red coral were the chief articles of sale.   On the
beach were some canoes with tall figure-heads curiously
carved and painted.

Weighed again at 2 P.M., and carried out the quarterly
firing during the afternoon.

7th.—Cruising off Lepers' Island, or Aoba.   Sent a
boat ashore at two places, the ship remaining under
way all the time ; at the latter place a French trader
was supplied with medicines, &c.

We had now left the part of the group which is
worked by the New Hebrides Mission ; Lepers' Island,
Aurora, Pentecost, and Ambrym are under the care of
the Melanesian Mission.   We were not, however, for-

tunate enough to fall in with their mission vessel, the
Southern Cross, although she had been in the neighbourhood a few days previously.

8th.—Cruising off Pentecost (Aragh) ; communicated with the shore once or twice, but did not
anchor.

The following day we were cruising off Ambrym all
the morning. Communicated with the shore once or
twice, and with trading vessels, but did not anchor.
Heavy clouds surrounded the lofty hills in the centre
of the island, but the lower ground was quite clear.

There is a great volcano in Ambrym, with a crater
which it is thought may possibly exceed in size even
Kilauea in Hawaii. No white man, however, has made
the ascent, and the natives have too great a dread of
the place to do so.

About noon we left Ambrym, and steamed across to
Port Sandwich, arriving at our destination about 4 P.M.
We found the *Saône* in harbour; but the *Swinger*, which
was to bring our mails from Noumea, had not yet
arrived. The following morning was occupied with
manning and arming boats, firing, &c. We found the
heat very oppressive, as the anchorage was completely
sheltered from any wind there might be outside.

The *Swinger* arrived from Noumea about 1 P.M. on
August 11th, bringing mails which were very welcome.
Earlier in the day a labour schooner arrived, bringing
news of a distressed ship at Havannah Harbour. We
sailed for that port at 5 P.M.

12th.—Arrived at Havannah Harbour, Efate, at 8
A.M.; found there the three-masted schooner *George
Noble*, of Sydney, laden with copra, last from the Gilbert

Group. The captain and three of the crew had died, apparently from poisoning; several others had also been very ill, but were now on the mend. They were, however, very glad of medicines and medical advice. We sailed at 5 P.M. for Noumea, and after a calm passage arrived at that port on August 15th, and received English mails of June 3rd.

Ships in harbour were the armed transport *Magellan*, a modern ship built of iron, but in shape and appearance like an old two-decker, and the gun-vessel *Volta*. The *Magellan* was employed in conveying convicts to and from Noumea, the Isle of Pines, and other convict stations. A fortnight at Noumea was very acceptable after a cruise in the New Hebrides. The weather, though warm, was very pleasant. Tennis, cricket, and good walks were to be had on shore, and pleasant excursions could be made to La Coulée and other places. At La Coulée there was a pretty little river, with some fine deep pools, which made first-rate bathing-places. In one of these there was a hot spring which afforded a very pleasant warm bath.

In the hills near La Coulée was a chrome mine, which was being energetically worked under the superintendence of a Scotch manager. The mine is at a height of 1,500 feet above the sea. The bags of chrome are sent down on two cables, one 1,000 yards long and the other 1,300 yards, and travel on rollers at the rate of about forty miles an hour. The speed is reduced as the gradient of the cable changes, but a strong buffer of hay is necessary to stop the bags. Gold, nickel, and copper are also found in the hills of New Caledonia, but mining has not as yet been a very profitable employ-

ment. The island is about 250 miles long, with an
average breadth of forty miles, and its area is about
6,000 square miles. It is very mountainous, rising in
some places to nearly 6,000 feet. The scenery is generally picturesque and pleasing; the valleys are densely
wooded, and produce many valuable trees, such as
cocoa-nut, bread-fruit, mango, and banana. The
country in the neighbourhood of Noumea is very like
that near Adelaide, except that the hills are higher
and more finely shaped than in Australia.

The French took possession of New Caledonia in
1853. Since then the natives, who probably belong to
the Papuan race, have rapidly decreased in numbers,
the present native population being under 30,000.

The colony does not appear to have much attraction
for French free settlers, and is still little more than a
penal settlement; nearly all the free French residents
hold official positions in the garrison or the penitentiary. There are about 11,000 convicts in New
Caledonia and the Isle of Pines. The large majority of
these are in the neighbourhood of Noumea; the principal convict establishment is at Ile Non, where a very
interesting afternoon was spent, going over the prison
buildings. There were workshops of all kinds—blacksmiths' shops, carpenters' shops, tailors', shoemakers',
&c., brick-fields, a small establishment where common pottery was turned out, and fine quarries, which
employed a large number of men. The solitary cells
were very gruesome places; the prisoners in the con-
demned cells, on the other hand, were much better off,
and were allowed many privileges. The whole place
appeared in excellent order. The food was good and

I

tolerably plentiful. The most cheerful individual we
met in the course of the afternoon was the executioner,
who displayed his guillotine with great pride, and remarked regretfully that times had been slack lately—
there had been scarcely any executions. A building
of ecclesiastical appearance held all manner of stores
for the use of the establishment. It was originally
intended for a church, but when completed was considered *too good* for that purpose, and was accordingly
utilized as a store.

The governor of the penitentiary was most polite
and obliging, freely showing whatever of interest there
was to be seen.

One or two dances and other entertainments were
given by residents on shore during our stay, and on
August 29th the captain and officers gave an afternoon
dance on board. About eighty people came, the majority of whom were French. The day was fine and
cool, and the dancing on the quarter-deck and poop
seemed to be much enjoyed, and was carried on with
great spirit.

On September 2nd a cricket match, *Calliope v.*
Noumea, resulted in a victory for the shore eleven.

According to our programme we were to wait for the
mail, which was due on September 3rd, and immediately after its arrival sail for the New Hebrides, to pay
another round of visits at the different islands. When
the mail actually arrived, a day late, on September 4th,
all this was changed by important and very welcome
news. The *Calliope* was ordered home, in order to pay
off and be repaired at Portsmouth, and was to proceed
at once to Sydney, in order to reach that port before

the departure of Admiral Fairfax, who had been appointed Second Naval Lord of the Admiralty. The afternoon was occupied with farewell visits and other preparations for departure, and the following morning at 9 A.M. we sailed, not for the New Hebrides, as we had expected, but for Sydney. The *Swinger*, *Volta*, *Saône*, and *Magellan* cheered ship as we passed, by way of wishing us a pleasant passage home. The irritation against things English, which had been so perceptible on our arrival, seemed now forgotten, and the *Calliope* was undoubtedly a popular ship in Noumea.

For the first two days after leaving Noumea we experienced strong head winds and made slow progress; but on the 9th we fell in with a strong northerly wind, and on the 10th made good 294 miles, which was so far the best day's run since commissioning.

We arrived at Sydney about 10 A.M. on September 11th, and found the *Orlando* and *Rapid* in Farm Cove. In the evening a large ball was held at the Darling-hurst Skating Rink, under the patronage of Mrs. Fairfax, in aid of the funds for furnishing the new Sailors' Home. It was very largely attended, and proved a great success both financially and socially.

On September 12th Rear-Admiral Fairfax gave up the command of the Australian Squadron. In the forenoon he visited all the men-of-war in harbour, and left for Melbourne by the 5 o'clock train. Six lieutenants of the fleet rowed the admiral's galley, containing Admiral and Mrs. Fairfax, from Admiralty House to Man-of-War Steps.

The remaining days at Sydney were fully occupied

with refitting and provisioning the ship, coaling, giving
leave, and all necessary preparations for a long voyage.
On the 12th and two following days, a wild-flower show
was held at Manby in aid of various Church works
in the town. A beautiful collection of all kinds of
Australian flowers was disposed in prettily decked
stalls presided over by ladies of the neighbourhood.
Most conspicuous were the handsome red waratahs, the
national flower of New South Wales, while graceful
rock lilies, and flannel flowers formed a pleasing contrast.

On September 15th H.M.S. *Lizard* and the French
gun-vessel *Volta* arrived ; and on September 21st H.M.S.
Opal arrived. On September 26th the captain and officers
of the *Orlando* gave a farewell dinner to the captain and
officers of the *Calliope ;* the *Orlando* was very prettily
decorated, temporary rockeries and fountains lighted
by small incandescent lamps producing a very pleasing
effect.

The last few days of September were much occupied
with farewell visits. Although the prospect of a speedy
return to England was a very pleasant one, yet much
regret was felt at leaving a pleasant station and many
kind friends.

October 2nd was the day fixed for beginning the
homeward voyage. During the morning and afternoon
numbers of friends came off to wish us good-bye ; and
amongst them Mr. Robertson of Eromanga.

By 4 P.M. all was ready, and the ship slipped from
her buoy and proceeded slowly down the harbour,
receiving a most enthusiastic " send-off." This day,
and April 4th, on which we arrived from Samoa,
are two days long to be remembered in connection

with Sydney. The following account of the departure
of the *Calliope* appeared in the *Sydney Morning
Herald* of October 3rd, and is a good though rather
florid description of what took place :—

" Just to give her a cheer took thousands of well-dressed
people out yesterday afternoon, and down to where
the famous *Calliope* was lying, with her homeward-
bound streamer flying at the main, and ready to
cast off from her moorings in Farm Cove. Standing
ashore immediately opposite to where she was lying,
and looking away out along the foreshore to the extreme
point of Fort Macquarie on the one side and as far
as Lady Macquarie's Chair to the right, might be
seen an almost unbroken line of spectators, all testi-
fying their appreciation of the good ship by waving
hats and handkerchiefs, or cheering to the echo the
gallant blue-jackets who hung in clusters to the
ratlines or waved their hats and lustily cheered from
the *Calliope's* shrouds. The situation of Farm Cove
is eminently suited to a demonstration, and the surroundings, including the Botanic Gardens, the Domain,
and the Fort, are so beautiful in themselves and
picturesque that on a fine day such as yesterday it was
not very surprising that an immense number of ladies
graced the shore with their presence, and, affixing their
handkerchiefs to parasol-tops, heartily joined in waving
an adieu to Captain Kane and his noble ship. In the
forenoon Lord Carrington and the Hon. Rupert Carrington paid a private visit to the ship, and Major-
General Edwards and some of the Marine Board and
harbour authorities also took leave of Captain Kane
and his officers on board.

" The scene amongst the blue-jackets on board was an animated one. The *Calliope's* sixteen ' dogs of war ' had been run in and snugly housed, ready for the homeward cruise. All the gear usually seen about the decks was clewed up, and everything clear for a fair start for Old England. Every sailor's face wore a broad smile, and some hearty shaking of hands went round as boat-load after boat-load of shore folk came and went. Such a collection of parrots, cockatoos, and birds of all kinds, presents from friends ashore, were to be seen stowed temporarily away in the first place to hand. There were shells from Samoa, native ornaments and curios from Fiji and the New Hebrides, and spears and poisoned arrows, dogs' teeth and sharks' teeth from the Solomons; in short, a veritable museum of South Sea Island novelties. There was no lack of enthusiasm on board the *Calliope* an hour before she left, but it is not unworthy of notice that a steadier body of men never left this or any other port. To whatever good influence or cause it may be attributed, it was remarked, not by one, but many visitors to the vessel, that intemperance in no single instance could be detected. Something more than the pleasure which the prospect of extra leave affords was apparently felt by the crew, but it was the pleasurable excitement of being surrounded by cheering crowds ashore and afloat, the playing of *Home, Sweet Home,* and similar airs by the various bands of music, and realizing that they and their handsome ship were the heroes of the hour. As 4 o'clock drew near, the time fixed for getting under way, a flotilla of watermen's boats ablaze with bunting put off from Fort Macquarie Point.

"Much credit is due to the licensed watermen who ply from Fort Macquarie for the good spirit with which they entered into the display. Their house at the Point was covered with flags and strings of flags stretched from point to point in such a way as to give a pretty appearance to the boat-landing. Each waterman also ran a line of small flags from stem to stern of his boat, and the effect of a large number so decorated was very pleasing. The demonstration was quite spontaneous on their part. Leaving the steps as mentioned, this flotilla fell into two lines, and passing H.M.S. *Lizard* made a circuit of the outgoing war-ship *Calliope*. Forming into processional order, and headed by a capital band carried on board a large cutter saved from the wreck of one of the American war-ships at Apia in the very storm in which the *Calliope* so distinguished herself, the watermen took a turn round the flag-ship, H.M.S. *Orlando*, and then fell into two lines out in mid-channel, one line towards Fort Denison, and the other towards Garden Island. In this position they formed a guard of honour, as the *Calliope* under very easy steam moved down the harbour. Precisely at 4 P.M. the bugle sounded on board the *Calliope*, and as quick as thought her yards were manned. This was the signal for immense cheering. From the bows of the *Lizard* close handy there was hearty cheering, and Farm Cove resounded again and again with the ringing echoes from the crews afloat, from the crowded pleasure steamers and the thousands who stretched from the shaded sloping point at Lady Macquarie's Chair to the extreme of Fort Macquarie. The order 'Slow ahead' went down to the *Calliope's* engine-room simultaneously with the manning of the yards, and the homeward voyage began.

"Doubtless there were some of the engineers, if no others, who, hearing this first order of the homeward-bound trip, would call to mind the day in Apia harbour, but a few months ago, when, dragging to within a fathom's length of the fatal coral reefs and the breakers, they heard the order, 'For God's sake give her every pound of steam,' and would contrast the two scenes for a moment. Directly the ship was under way the yards of the other ships were manned. The *Orlando* 'manned ship,' and continuous cheering followed the vessel down the harbour. Some fine music came from the band on the *Orlando*; and a band afloat, sent down to do honour to their departing comrades by H.M.S. *Opal*, at present at Fitzroy dock, took an active part in the 'send-off.' A number of harbour steamers, amongst which were noticed the *Pearl*, *Swansea*, *Atlanta*, and several launches, took part in the procession. On Government House lawn were His Excellency Lord Carrington and the Hon. Rupert Carrington and suite, joining very heartily in the waving of hats as the *Calliope* moved out of the Cove. When the vessel was out in mid-channel, the fine band on board the Orient liner R.M.S. *Orizaba*, Captain Conlan, struck up, and continued to play until the vessel rounded Bradley's Head, where the whistling of the steamers' 'Cock-a-doodle-doo,' and the hurrahs of the people afloat expended themselves, and Captain Kane signalled 'Farewell to the port.'"

HOMEWARD BOUND.

October 2*nd.*—The ship was now well filled, as we were taking home twenty-five invalids and time-expired men, and seven prisoners. We were also taking seven men to the *Dart*, as well as stores of various kinds for the *Dart* and *Rapid*, and a whaler for the *Dart*. At starting the weather was simply perfect—smooth sea, light winds, and bright sunshine; but in consequence of the strong southerly current we made but slow progress, and when on the following day we encountered a strong head wind, our progress became very slow indeed.

About 5 A.M. on the 4th, the *Orlando* passed us on her way to Moreton Bay.

In consequence of the bad weather, it became necessary for us to put into Moreton Bay for coal. We arrived on the 7th, and anchored about noon. Found the *Orlando* anchored in the bay. Moreton Bay, through which the Brisbane river is approached, is an extensive sheet of water, thirty-five miles long north and south, and thirteen miles broad; it is sheltered on its eastern side by Stradbroke and Moreton Islands. A great portion of the bay is encumbered by shoals.

We lay about two miles from the mouth of the Brisbane river, and about eighteen miles from the town of Brisbane. As the ship had only called in to coal, and was to leave again as soon as that operation was completed, no leave was given, and therefore Brisbane cannot be reckoned among the places visited by the *Calliope*. Coaling was completed on the 8th; and at daylight on the 9th we weighed and proceeded. The strong northerly wind had blown itself out, and with a fair wind and smooth sea, we averaged about 180' for the next few days.

On the afternoon of October 10th we once more entered the tropics, and saw quite as much of them as we wanted to in the next six months.

About 2 P.M. on the 13th we passed Cape Grafton, going through a narrow channel between the mainland and some pretty wooded islands. The whole coast-line in the neighbourhood of the cape was picturesque, and covered with dense vegetation ; the scenery was very similar to that of the New Hebrides.

Arrived at Cooktown at 9 A.M. on October 14th, and anchored in an open bay, about a mile and a half from the entrance to the harbour. H.M.S. *Raven* came out to receive stores, and was secured astern while the stores were being passed out. The colonial gun-boat *Paluma*, temporarily lent as tender to the *Orlando* for service on the Queensland Survey, also came out and anchored near us. In the afternoon both *Raven* and *Paluma* returned into harbour, cheering ship in farewell as they steamed away.

Cooktown, a rising town of about 8,000 inhabitants, is situated at the mouth of the Endeavour River, famed from its connection with the history of Captain Cook. A large proportion of the inhabitants are Chinese. Weighed at 5 A.M. on the following day, and proceeded to Lizard Island, where we were to meet the *Dart*. Anchored off Lizard Island about half-past eleven ; discharged men, boat, and stores to the *Dart* very rapidly, and sailed again about 1 P.M.

Lizard Island is a desolate-looking spot—not the place one would choose to spend Christmas at, as we afterwards heard it was the *Dart's* fate to do. It is much more conspicuous than most of the islands inside the Barrier Reef, rising to a height of nearly 1,200 feet.

About 7 P.M. we anchored under the lee of No. VI. Island, Howick Group. This group consists of ten small islands, distinguished, convict-fashion, by numbers, not by names. No. VI. is a low, bushy island, about two miles in circumference, and made a good break-water.

As we were now in the most troublesome part of the Barrier Reef, we anchored at night, both on the 16th and 17th, each time far away from any shelter, but in ten or twelve fathoms. At noon on October 18th, Cape York, the north point of Australia, bore due south, and we soon lost sight of the Southern Continent. By 3 P.M. we were through Torres Straits, and as we had a fair wind and plenty of coal, it was not necessary to coal at Thursday Island.

For many days after passing Torres Straits, as we steamed slowly through the Arafura and Flores Seas, the weather was perfectly calm, and the water like a mill-pond. The temperature was very high, but as all scuttles could be open, the heat was perfectly bearable. For some days we were out of sight of land, but on the 24th we sighted some small islands between Timor Laut and Timor. On the 25th we passed close to the northern coast of Timor, and from this point scarcely lost sight of land till we reached Singapore. On the 27th and 28th we were passing Flores, and about 9 A.M.

on October 29th the volcano of Tamborah, 12,000 feet
high, in the island of Sumbawa, bore due south. This
volcano, the largest active volcano in the world, was in
eruption in 1815, when the volcanic dust was carried as
far as Timor in one direction and Sumatra in the other,
over a district 1,500 miles long east and west by 900
miles north and south.

On the 30th we passed Lombok, on the following
day the island of Baly, and on November 1st and 2nd
were in sight of the northern coast of Java. A large
number of fishing-boats were at work in these waters,
and a sharp look-out had to be kept to avoid running
some of them down.

Entered Banka Strait about 6 P.M. on November 3rd,
and anchored for the night about 11 P.M.

Weighed early next morning, and passed through
Banka Strait, and passing Rhio Strait on the 5th,
arrived at Singapore at 9 A.M. on November 6th.
William Gill, A.B., an invalid who had been sent on
board at Sydney for passage home, and had been much
tried by the long passage and hot weather, died about
6 A.M. on the 6th, and was buried the following
morning. The funeral party left the ship at 6 A.M.
The cemetery is about four miles from the Tanjong
Pagar wharf, on the opposite side of the town. It is
nicely planted with trees and shrubs, but is badly
situated, as there seems to be no means of draining off
the water after rains. The *Orion* was in harbour when
we arrived ; she was stationed at Singapore while the
land defences were being constructed, but as these have
now been completed and armed, her presence is no longer
necessary, and she has since returned to the Mediter-

ranean. We at once went alongside the Tanjong Pagar wharf, and remained snugly tied up during our stay at Singapore.

Coaling began about 1 P.M. and continued till midnight, recommenced the following morning, and was completed shortly before noon, when 370 tons had been taken in. The coolies put the coal on board wonderfully quickly, but stowing and trimming are lengthy operations. While we remained alongside, the wharf was crowded by a number of traders in all kinds of goods—fruit, Malacca canes, silk handkerchiefs, Japanese cabinets, &c.

The wharf is about two miles from the centre of the town, which can be reached either by tram or "jin-ricksha," or in a small carriage known as a "gharry," which is by far the pleasantest way. The road to the town is uninteresting, the houses being mean-looking and straggling, but the town itself is full of life and interest. Shops of all kinds, with Chinese, Japanese, and Indian wares, are very tempting. There are some pretty drives in the neighbourhood, especially to the Botanical Gardens, close to the Targlin Barracks, where an infantry regiment is quartered. The gardens are beautifully kept, and contain many curious plants; the most noticeable were the beautiful, delicate lace-plant, and the Victoria Regia, a magnificent water-lily, discovered in 1837 in British Guiana, and named after Queen Victoria, the leaves of which rest on the water like large flat trays, six feet in diameter. There are also some Chinese pleasure gardens, which are held in great estimation by the natives, but are rather curious than pretty. They are intensely artificial; all the shrubs are trained on wire frames into the shape of dragons or other strange beasts. From the Artillery Barracks at Fort Canning a very fine view of the town and harbour can be obtained.

Government House is prettily situated on rising ground on the outskirts of the town. During our stay the Governor, Sir Cecil Clementi Smith, K.C.M.G., held an afternoon reception, which was largely attended by the residents.

Singapore has every appearance of a flourishing place with a great future before it. The population of the island is at present about 155,000, made up of all nations. The island is about twenty-seven miles long by fourteen wide, and is separated from the Malay peninsula by a narrow strait about three-quarters of a mile wide. It was occupied by Sir Stamford Raffles in 1819, and ceded to the British Government by the Sultan of Johore in 1824. Singapore is one of the greatest trading ports in the world. In 1887 over 3,400 ships, with a tonnage of more than 2,600,000, entered the harbour.

We sailed at 10 A.M. on November 9th, having thoroughly enjoyed a few days in harbour after the long cruise from Sydney. We went out through the New Harbour, getting a sight of some of the recently constructed fortifications as we passed. We were clear of the Narrows soon after noon, when the pilot left the ship.

On our way through the Straits of Malacca we came in for several heavy rain-squalls, but otherwise the weather was favourable. On November 12th, while still in the Straits, we passed a Turkish war-ship, and were rather puzzled to know what she could be doing in this part of the world.

We heard some news of her at Colombo and Aden, and afterwards were interested by seeing the following paragraph in one of our weekly papers :—

" *The Troubles of a Turkish War-ship.*—The London correspondent of the *Manchester Guardian* writes : ' A curious story comes to me from the East of the voyage of a Turkish war-ship from Constantinople to Japan, conveying to the Mikado a decoration from the Sultan. It is now over nine months since the *Erzegroul*, as the vessel is called, left the Bosphorus. She had broken down three or four times—once in the Suez Canal— and she has been delayed in every port she entered by the want of funds. She was delayed at Aden for weeks, and at Colombo for three months. At last she got as far as Singapore, but the voyage so far having been un- expectedly long, her ammunition had given out, and she was unable to fire the usual salute to the port. Accordingly the Governor gave orders that, an explana- tion having been given of this discourtesy, she was not to be treated as a man-of-war, and the port dues were demanded ; but the captain had no money for the pur- pose, and was equally unable to purchase the necessary coals to enable the vessel to proceed to Japan. He had when the last mail left been some months in Singapore waiting for remittances from Constantinople, which either never came or did not come in sufficient time.. I believe the ship is still at Singapore.' "

We passed Acheen Head about 8 A.M. on November 13th, and for the next few days were favoured with a light breeze and smooth sea; but on the 16th there was a

complete change. Strong winds from the south-west,
with a good deal of rain and thick weather prevailed,
and a lumpy sea reduced the speed of the ship considerably. In addition to this, strong currents were experienced. We arrived at Colombo about 4 P.M. on
the 20th, and moored in the snug harbour. We found
that the bad weather was due to a cyclone in the Bay
of Bengal, and that mail-steamers had been delayed
as much as ourselves. In fact one mail-boat had
experienced strong currents, first to the southward and
then to the northward, on succeeding days, and, owing
to the thick weather, had actually overshot her mark,
and found herself about thirty miles north of Colombo
when she made the land. The Orient liner *Cuzco* was
in harbour when we arrived, and sailed soon afterwards
for Australia. She was taking out part of the relief
crew for the *Egeria*.

There are plenty of interesting sights in Colombo
to occupy three or four days very pleasantly. The
Hindu and Buddhist temples are worth a visit. A
drive through the narrow streets of the native parts
of the town, and through pretty shady roads on the
outskirts, where one village succeeds another in quick
succession, gives some idea of the size of Colombo,
which has now a population of nearly 120,000. A
long row of shops near the landing-place, where curios
of all kinds are displayed, proves very dangerous to the
pockets of visitors. Ceylon is noted for its precious
stones of all kinds, especially cats'-eyes and rubies.

A most interesting excursion can be made to Kandy;
this can be done in one day, but it is far more enjoyable to take two days for the trip if possible. Kandy,

the old capital of Ceylon, is connected with Colombo
by a charming line of rail seventy-three miles in length,
which, for many miles, winds among the lofty hills
amongst which Kandy is situated. Bold hills and
fertile valleys succeed one another in quick succession,
and in parts the railway line runs along the side of
precipitous cliffs with overhanging rocks seeming to
threaten destruction from above, on the one hand, and
a sheer drop to the valley beneath on the other. The
town is situated in a pretty valley, surrounded by lofty
hills : a small lake adds much to the beauty of the
scene.

The great Buddhist Temple, where the sacred tooth
of Buddha is kept in a jewelled shrine, is the great
lion of the place ; but the Oriental Library, and the
Palace of the Kings of Kandy, are full of interest.
Ceylon has been occupied successively by the Portuguese, the Dutch, and the English. The Portuguese
landed in the island as far back as 1507, but about
150 years later were dispossessed by the Dutch, who,
in their turn, had to give way to the English in 1796
In 1801 Ceylon became a separate Crown colony, but
still the Kings of Kandy retained their independence,
and it was not till 1815 that the last King of Kandy
was deposed and banished. About two miles from
Kandy are some beautiful botanical gardens, where
all kinds of tropical plants flourish in great abundance ;
amongst others the deadly upas tree, and the all-
spice tree. Near these gardens was a flourishing tea-
plantation and factory, where tea was to be seen in all
stages of its preparation.

We sailed at 5 P.M. on November 24th, and for a

K

time experienced light westerly winds, bur on the 28th
the wind shifted to the N.E., at first light, but gradually
increasing in strength. The last point of Socotra was
abeam about 7 A.M. on December 3rd, and during the
day we were running along the north coast of the
island at a distance of twelve or fourteen miles.

Socotra, seen from the northward, appears a most
desolate and uninviting country, with great heaps of
gleaming sand swept up by the monsoon, stretching
far up the cliffs. The island of Socotra is about 100
miles long from E. to W., with an extreme breadth
of forty miles; it formerly belonged to the Sultan of
Kishu in Arabia, but in 1886 was taken under British
protection.

Arrived at Aden at 4 A.M. on December 6th, and
anchored off Steamer Point. Found here *Ranger* and
Pigeon.

A French steamer lay sunk in the bay with her
masts and funnel above water : a melancholy sight.

Almost the only excursion that can be made in Aden
is a visit to the Tanks, which are certainly a very fine
work, and have a total capacity of 10,000,000 gallons.
At the time of our visit they did not contain a drop
of water, and this is their usual condition, as rain is
very rare in Aden ; it is said that it rains here once
in three years. A line of old fortifications on the land
side, and a number of powerful new batteries commanding the bay and its approaches, are interesting.
A good deal of exercise may be taken in a short time
by walking to the signal station on Jebel Sham-Shan,
1,600 feet high, reached by a steep and rather rough
path. From the top a very fine view of the harbour

and surrounding country is obtained. Aden became a British possession in 1839, and since then very much seems to have been done to make it tolerably habitable; but the total absence of grass and trees is a defect which apparently no ingenuity can overcome.

Nothing is manufactured in Aden except water and salt; but very fine ostrich feathers can be bought, and curious Somali baskets of coloured grasses are worth getting.

Brig.-General Hogg, C.B., the Resident, visited the ship on the 7th, and was saluted on leaving with thirteen guns.

Sailed about 5 P.M. on December 8th.

December 9th.—Sighted Perim light soon after midnight, and passed through the strait about 5 A.M. About 4.30 P.M. passed H.M.S. *Malabar* outward bound.

Passed the Dædalus light shortly before midnight on the 13th, and passed the Brothers during the afternoon of the 14th.

Arrived at Suez about 10 A.M. on December 16th. Since the P. and O. steamers have discontinued calling at Suez the prosperity of the place has diminished. The Suez Hotel, once a flourishing concern, was closed a few days after we passed through.

Suez is noted for its donkeys, which are named after various celebrities of the day; and very good fun can be got out of a ride on "Mr. Gladstone" or "Mrs. Langtry."

From Suez a party was made up to visit Cairo, and join the ship again at Port Said. The night journey from Suez to Cairo was long and wearisome, but this was soon forgotten in the interest of seeing the bazaars and

K 2

mosques of Cairo, and of climbing to the top of the great Pyramid, penetrating to the king's chamber, and standing between the paws of the Sphinx.

On the return journey to Ismailia, the railway passes through the lines of Tel-el-Kebir, where the trenches are still plainly visible.

The ship entered the Canal on December 17th at 7 A.M., and anchored for the night in the basin at Ismailia. Proceeded again next morning, and gared up for the night about fifteen miles from Port Said. Passed H.M.S. *Crocodile* in the Canal. Arrived at Port Said about 11 A.M. on December 19th, and made fast to buoys. Once through the canal we began to think we were getting near home, but our calculations were altogether thrown out by the receipt of telegraphic orders to proceed at once to Aden. No reason for this change of plans was given, but we guessed correctly that it was owing to the difficulty with Portugal.

Coaling ship began at once and proceeded with the vigour usual at Port Said, and at the same time all necessary arrangements for our return voyage were being carried out. Invalids, time expired men, and prisoners were discharged to the *Melita* for passage to England, and at 9 A.M. on the 20th we once more entered the Canal with the ship's head turned the wrong way, and no one feeling particularly cheerful at the prospect of an indefinite sojourn at Aden or Zanzibar. Reached Ismailia the same evening, using our electric search lights for the last half-hour. Met in the Canal the merchant steamer *Calliope*.

December 21st, Suez.—Arrived at Suez about 5 P.M. on December 21st, having been twice through the

Canal in five days: an unusual experience for any ship.

At Suez we rapidly took in supplies of bread, beef, and vegetables, and proceeded at once for Aden. Christmas Day was spent in the Red Sea: some rain fell in the morning, but the day proved fine and calm. There was not much to remind any one of an English Christmas, and the day was spent quietly. There were the usual services in the morning, and the customary freedom of singing on the lower deck throughout the afternoon. In the evening the captain and warrant-officers dined in the ward-room.

Passed Perim Light at 10.30 A.M. on the 28th, and arrived at Aden at 8 A.M. on Sunday, the 29th. Here we found orders to proceed to Zanzibar as soon as possible. Sunday routine was "belayed" and coaling began immediately. Took on board a thirty-seven foot steam pinnace, machine guns, and ammunition, for conveyance to Zanzibar. We were obliged to wait for the mail which was bringing out charts of the East Coast of Africa, and immediately these were received, we sailed for Zanzibar at 2 P.M. on December 31st. The *Satellite*, homeward-bound from China, had also been ordered to Zanzibar, and had left Aden on December 28th. Thus we saw another old year out at sea, instead of welcoming 1890 as we had anticipated, while snugly anchored at Malta.

1890.

THE EAST COAST OF AFRICA.

January 1st.—After leaving Aden we experienced
fine weather and light head winds, and averaging
about nine knots passed Cape Guardafui about 8 A.M.
on the 2nd. From this point we had fair winds and
a favourable current till about 2° S. lat., and made good
runs each day, the best being 300′ on January 4th.

After a pleasant and quick passage we arrived at
Zanzibar about 1 P.M. on January 7th. The *Satellite*
had arrived earlier in the day. Found here in addition
to the *Satellite*, the *Boadicea*, flagship of Rear-Admiral
Sir E. R. Freemantle, K.C.B., C.M.G., the Commander-
in-Chief on the East Indies Station, *Reindeer*, *Algerine*,
Pigeon, and *Stork*. Also the German gun-vessels
Sperber and *Schwalbe*, and the French gun-boat *Bouvet*,
which not long before had narrowly escaped becoming
a total wreck a few miles to the southward of Zanzibar.
Later in the day the *Turquoise* arrived. Hoisted out
the steam pinnace and other cargo which had crowded
our eck during the passage from Aden.

Zanzibar from the sea looks quite an imposing place.
The Sultan's Palace, Clock Tower, British Consulate,
German Consulate, Cathedral, and other large buildings

make a good show; but as soon as one has landed the illusion is dispelled. The streets are very narrow, very crooked, and very dirty, even in the European parts of the town, and in the native streets the same may be said still more strongly.

The houses are crowded very closely together, and although the town does not occupy much ground the population is said to be about 80,000. Many of the larger houses have very handsome doors of carved wood, with peculiar fastenings in place of locks and bolts. One of the most remarkable buildings in Zanzibar is the Cathedral of the Universities' Mission to Central Africa, which was built between 1873 and 1879, according to the plans and under the superintendence of the late Bishop Steere.

The cathedral is constructed of coral, and is, considering the material, a really remarkable work; it stands on what was formerly the great slave-market of Zanzibar. Close to the cathedral is the Mkimazini Mission House, where several of the mission workers live, and where there is a school for freed slaves' boys. Near by is a colony of married freed slaves. At Kuingani, two miles from Zanzibar, is another mission house, where there is a school and training-college for older lads. And two miles further on, along the shores of the bay, is Mbwein, where there is a village of freed slaves and a pretty church, and, close at hand, a third mission house, where there is a large girls' school, conducted by a number of the hard-working ladies of the Mission. It was interesting to be told at Kuingani that the pupils there send contributions to aid in the education of a Melanesian boy at Norfolk Island; and receive from the distant Pacific Island similar help for their own work. As far as could be judged from a short stay in Zanzibar, the mission is doing a good and sorely-needed work among the freed slaves who are brought to the island.

January 8th.—The admiral came on board for a short time in the morning.

On the 9th half-masted ensign and fired minute-guns for the death of the Dowager-Empress Augusta of Germany. Coaling ship all day; a slow process, carried on by the natives, both men and women, who sing a monotonous sort of dirge all the time they are at work.

On the following day we were ordered to man and provision the steam pinnace which we had brought from Aden. She was manned by seven of our men and two seedies, under the command of a warrant-officer, and sailed the next morning in company with two other boats to cruise off Pemba on the look-out for slave dhows. We took on board sixteen seedies and three interpreters; the former were very useful, but the latter had a very easy time of it while they remained on board. H.M.S. *Garnet* arrived on the 10th.

On the morning of January 10th the Sultan of Zanzibar held a *levée*, which was attended by many officers from the fleet. Coffee and sherbet were provided for the visitors.

On January 11th the fleet sailed at 8.30 A.M. for the southward. Our destination was known only to the admiral, but everything was ordered to be in complete readiness for active service, and landing parties were told off and provided with all necessaries. The *Stork* returned to Zanzibar after a few hours; the afternoon was occupied with exercising at steam tactics; and at 5 P.M. the *Garnet* parted company and returned to Zanzibar.

Shortly before noon on the following day the admiral made a signal to the effect that there was no likelihood of active operations, as a satisfactory termination of the negotiations with Portugal had been arrived at; and that we were on our way to meet the Cape squadron off Pomba Bay.

On January 13th the fleet was sailing in extended order looking out for the Cape ships. About 6 P.M. they were sighted and soon afterwards we turned northwards once more and steamed slowly towards Zanzibar. About 11 P.M. the *Raleigh, Curaçoa, Brisk,* and *Kingfisher* joined company. Admiral Wells was not on board his flagship, as he had remained at the Cape.

The next three days were fully occupied with steam tactics and drills of all kinds. Arrived at Zanzibar about 8.30 A.M. on January 17th. We were not sorry to get a few days quietly in harbour after so much steam tactics and drill. Although the town of Zanzibar does not offer many attractions, yet the country behind it is pretty, and a good lawn tennis ground and a fair cricket ground are within easy distance.

On January 18th H.M.S. *Conquest* arrived : she had just been sent from China to be temporarily attached to the East Indies station, and her people were naturally not much pleased at the change. The combined fleet now numbered fourteen ships, viz., *Boadicea, Turquoise, Garnet, Cossack, Kingfisher, Reindeer, Pigeon, Algerine,*

and *Conquest*, belonging to the East Indies Station;
Raleigh, *Curaçoa*, and *Brisk* from the Cape, and *Satellite* and *Calliope* homeward bound.

On January 24th, the sailing regatta for boats of the
combined fleet was held. The wind was light and
variable and none of our boats succeeded in taking
prize. On the following day, however, when the
rowing regatta took place it was quite a different
story, and our Sydney-built cutter and whaler, which
replaced our boats lost at Samoa, gave a good account
of themselves. Altogether our boats took six first
prizes in the following races : cutters, bluejackets ;
cutters, marines ; whalers, bluejackets ; whalers, stokers
and idlers ; whalers, officers ; and dingies. The dis-
tinguishing flag of the *Calliope's* boats was the four
stars of the Southern Cross on a blue ground ; in
addition to this allusion to our old station, after each
race in which the cutter came in first, her crew displayed
a large white flag on which was painted a kangaroo,
with the New South Wales motto, " Advance Australia."
On the morning of the same day a most interesting
service was held in the Cathedral, when the Rev. Cecil
Majaliwa, the first native priest, was ordained by
Bishop Smythies for work in the mission stations on
the mainland.

On January 28th a sham fight and review took
place on shore. The marines of the fleet landed
at 5 A.M. and took up a position commanding the
beach, which was afterwards attacked and carried by
bodies of seamen supported by the fire of the *Pigeon* and
Reindeer. A march past before the admiral and sultan
followed, and every one was on board again soon after

nine. In the afternoon there was a large gathering of the mission school children at Mbwein, which was attended by the admiral and many officers from the fleet, and seemed to be thoroughly enjoyed by the children.

The *Raleigh* and *Curaçoa* sailed for the Cape at 8 A.M. on January 29th, and the remainder of the fleet, with the exception of the *Algerine* and *Pigeon*, sailed for Mombasa about 2 P.M. The Consul-General, Colonel Euan Smith, took passage in the *Boadicea*. The afternoon was occupied with steam tactics, and the fleet anchored for the night in Cocotoni Bay at the north end of Zanzibar. Weighed early next morning, occupied the day in steam tactics and anchored for the night in Funsi Bay on the African coast.

Arrived off Mombasa about 1.30 P.M. on January 31st. The island of Mombasa separates two fine harbours, the northern harbour is Mombasa, and the southern is Port Reitz. As the entrance to Port Reitz is rather intricate, the two divisions of the fleet entered separately, and anchored in two lines ; the *Cossack* and *Brisk* entered shortly afterwards and formed a third line. Port Reitz is a fine land-locked harbour surrounded by tolerably high hills covered with trees and brushwood. It is likely to increase in importance as the East African Company are about to construct a railway, which may very possibly have its terminus on the shores of Port Reitz, instead of at the present town of Mombasa. There was a good beach for landing on the island of Mombasa about half a mile ahead of the ships, and a pleasant walk of three miles along well-marked paths brought one to the town with its mud houses and

teeming population. On the opposite side of the
harbour, about a mile from Mombasa, is Freretown, the
flourishing settlement of the Church Missionary Society's
Mission, where a colony of freed slaves is cared for by
the hard-working missionaries, and good schools are
provided both for girls and boys. The doctor, who
gives his services to the mission, has evidently
plenty of work on his hands, as the natives are
subject to most ghastly and obstinate sores.

During our stay in Port Reitz the torpedo depart-
ments of all the ships were employed in laying down
mine-fields, &c. A good deal of shooting was obtained
in the neighbourhood ; guinea-fowl, partridge, quail,
and pigeon were plentiful on the mainland, but game
was scarce in the island. The curious baobab or mon-
key-bread trees were very numerous ; one magnificent
specimen, of which a photograph was obtained, had a
trunk more than one hundred feet in circumference. It
has been calculated that one of these trees, fourteen feet
in diameter, must be a thousand years old, and that a tree
thirty feet in diameter must be about five thousand years
old. The fruit is oblong and hangs like a pendant ; the
interior of the fruit is something like ginger-bread in
appearance, with a pleasant acid flavour.

The harbour was quite free from sharks, and "hands
to bathe " was piped both morning and evening.

On February 1st the *Boadicea* sailed for Zanzibar,
having on board the consul-general. She returned to
Port Reitz on the 4th.

About 2 P.M. on February 7th the fleet weighed and
sailed for the northward. Arrived off Malindi about
7 A.M. on the 8th, and anchored in an open roadstead

encumbered with numerous reefs. We could see the small town about a couple of miles from our anchorage ; there appeared to be few houses of any size.

The Wali, or Governor of Malindi, under the Sultan of Zanzibar, visited the *Boadicea, Turquoise,* and *Calliope.*

Malindi is famous as being the most northern point on the east coast of Africa reached by Vasco da Gama in his famous voyage round the Cape of Good Hope in 1498. On a point of land beyond the town we could see a pillar, which was set up by the great Portuguese navigator as a memorial of his visit, and which has lately been somewhat barbarously whitewashed to render it a conspicuous land-mark.

About 3 P.M. the *Pigeon* arrived from Zanzibar, bringing orders for the *Satellite* and ourselves to proceed to England. This was very welcome news to all on board, as we had seen quite as much of the East Indies station as we wanted to.

February 9th.—The fleet sailed at 6 P.M., and arrived at Manda Bay, near Lamu, about 7 A.M. next morning. This is a large bay sheltered by islands. A few houses and some cultivated land were to be seen on shore, but there seemed to be nothing very attractive and no one landed. At 7 A.M. on the 10th the fleet weighed, and as soon as we were outside the bay, the *Satellite* parted company homeward bound, receiving the usual farewell cheers as she steamed away to the northward. Half an hour later we also parted company with the fleet to make the best of our way to Zanzibar, there to coal and pick up our boat's crew.

Arrived at Zanzibar at 3 P.M. on the 11th. The rest

of the squadron arrived about six o'clock the same
evening, with the exception of the *Conquest*, which had
gone to Pemba to take a relief crew to the steam-pinnace
we had manned. The following day was fully occupied
with coaling.

February 13*th.*—About 1 A.M. on February 13th our
cruising steam-pinnace's crew returned, bringing the
news that the *Conquest* was ashore off Pemba. She
only remained aground a few hours, and was floated off
uninjured at the next high tide. The same day, about
1 P.M., Seyyid Khalifa, Sultan of Zanzibar, died suddenly. His was a short reign, as he only succeeded his
brother in 1888. There was some fear of rioting among
the Arabs, as until the succession of Khalifa, riots had
always occurred on the death of a sultan. The *Reindeer*
and *Pigeon* moved up close to the town into positions
protecting the British Consulate, and the marines were
in readiness for landing in case of any disturbance.
Nothing of the kind, however, was needed, as the
funeral of the late sultan and the proclamation of his
brother Ali as his successor was carried out without
interruption, and no disturbance of any kind took place
during the night.

On February 14th we discharged our interpreter and
seedies. Invalids and time-expired men from the other
ships joined for passage to England. The *Conquest*
arrived at 8 A.M.

On the morning of the 15th the Commander-in-Chief
came on board for a few minutes to wish good-bye;
the Consul-General also came to pay a short farewell
visit. At 9.15 A.M., with the long homeward-bound
pennant flying once more, we weighed and steamed

round the fleet exchanging farewell cheers with each ship as we passed. By ten o'clock we were fairly on our way, and saw the last of Zanzibar without much regret being expressed by any one on board.

For the first two days we experienced strong head winds, a lumpy sea, and strong southerly current, and made but slow progress in consequence. On the 18th, however, the wind and sea moderated. On the 19th crossed the line for the sixth time since commissioning. Passed Cape Guardafui on the 23rd, and reached Aden about 10.30 A.M. on February 25th. We were surprised to find that the *Satellite*, which had very nearly a week's start of ourselves, had not yet arrived. We heard afterwards that in consequence of the strong northerly wind she ran short of coal and was obliged to run for the Seychelles, and eventually arrived at Aden the day after we left. The P. and O. s.s. *Coromandel* was in harbour when we arrived ; amongst her passengers were Bishop and Mrs. Selwyn, whom we had last seen at Norfolk Island. They were now returning to Australia after a short visit to England.

We sailed at 5 P.M. on the 27th, and were glad to find a fair wind and calm sea outside; passed Perim about 5 A.M. on the 28th.

Calm weather, and an uneventful passage. Passed H.M.S. *Malabar* outward-bound on March 2nd. Passed the Dædalus light at 6 P.M. on the 5th, and arrived at Suez at 3 P.M. on the 8th. Anchored in the roads for the night. Found here H.M.S. *Crocodile* which sailed for Bombay soon after our arrival. Entered the Canal at 8 A.M. on March 9th, and got as far as "Guillaume Gare," only ten miles from Suez, where we were detained

in consequence of a dhow laden with stones having sunk
in the Canal near Chalouf by a collision with the Messa-
geries Maritimes company's steamer *Australien.* We
were able to start again about noon on the 10th, and
had a clear run to Ismailia, which we reached about
5.30, and anchored in the basin for the night. Made
an early start next morning, and were obliged to "gare
up" at the first siding after leaving Ismailia, but after
that had a clear run, and reached Port Said at 3 P.M.
Found the *Albacore* in harbour.

Completed coaling ship at noon on the 12th, and
sailed at 3 P.M. for Malta. Once outside the shelter of
the breakwater we met a strong south-westerly wind
and considerable sea.

We arrived at Malta about 10 A.M. on March 19th,
and were very pleased to find ourselves snugly moored
in Dockyard Creek, after a rough night outside. Found
here the greater part of the Mediterranean fleet, the *Cam-
perdown* (temporary flag-ship of Vice-Admiral Sir
Anthony Hiley Hoskins, K.C.B., Commander-in-Chief),
*Benbow, Edinburgh, Colossus, Téméraire, Agamemnon,
Orion, Australia, Phaeton, Polyphemus, Carysfort, Surprise, Cruiser, Scout, and Fearless.* Also the *Merlin*
homeward-bound, and the troopship *Tamar* about to
start for England.

The sight of so many modern ships like the *Cam-
perdown, Benbow,* &c., with their enormous guns, gave a
very strong impression of the rapid changes which have
taken place in the navy in the last few years. The
ship was soon surrounded by a crowd of dhysoes and
tradesmen eager for custom. Coaling ship began
shortly after our arrival, and was completed the same

evening. On the following days general leave was given to both watches; and it is satisfactory to note that there was not a single instance of leave-breaking. For those who were strangers to Malta, there was much to be seen, both in Valetta and the neighbourhood. The ancient armoury in the Governor's Palace and the Council Chamber with its beautiful tapestry, were amongst the first places visited.

The drive to the old capital Citta Vechia had attractions for a good many; the remains of the Roman villa there, now carefully preserved, were well worth a visit, as were also the ancient catacombs at Rabato, whose origin is a point of dispute. One of the most noticeable objects in the island is the large dome of the church at Musta. This dome has a greater diameter than that of St. Paul's Cathedral; the dome of Musta Church is 117 feet in diameter, and St. Paul's 107, but the Cathedral dome is higher and far more graceful than that of the Maltese architect. It is a curious fact that the present church was built over the original church at Musta, which was removed as soon as the new building was completed.

All the roads and fields are enclosed by high stone walls; and looking at the country from a valley one sees nothing but these walls, and the whole place looks barren in the extreme; but looking down from an eminence over the surrounding low country one sees the very large amount of cultivated and very fertile soil which makes Malta deserve the name proudly given to it by its inhabitants, *Fior del Mondo*—"The Flower of the World." And one realizes the enormous amount of labour necessary to have transformed into

L

this fertile and populous island the almost barren
rock which was handed over to the Knights of St.
John in 1530. In 1887 the estimated population was,
Malta, 138,400; Gozo, 18,600. Thus Malta, with an
area of only ninety square miles, has a population of
over 1,450 per square mile, and is one of the most
densely populated countries in the world.

On March 21st the *Merlin* sailed for Gibraltar. On
March 22nd the *Edinburgh* sailed for Platea, and on
the same day the *Satellite* arrived from Port Said.

At 2 P.M. on March 24 we sailed for Gibraltar,
making sail as we went out of harbour. The *Téméraire*
and *Carysfort* had left the harbour a few minutes before
ourselves, and also made sail. We soon lost sight of
the other two as they were going eastward to Platea,
and we were bound for Gibraltar. Passed Pantalaria
about 2 P.M. on the 25th.

The passage was made partly under sail, and as the
wind was light proved rather long. Sighted the snow-
covered Sierra Nevada early on the morning of the 30th,
and ran along all day with a fair wind in sight of the
Spanish coast.

Arrived at Gibraltar about 10 A.M. on March 31st,
and anchored about two cables from the New Mole.

The morning was very thick, and we did not see the
Rock till within three or four miles of it ; later the fog
cleared away, but heavy clouds still surrounded the top
of the Rock. Found here, as we had expected, the
Undaunted and *Merlin*, and also unexpectedly the
Channel Fleet, consisting of *Northumberland*, *Anson*,
Monarch, *Iron Duke*, and *Curlew*. The *Curlew* was
proceeding out of harbour for target practice, as we

entered. And very shortly after our arrival the *Undaunted* sailed for Malta and the *Merlin* for England.

We only remained a few hours, long enough however to get our mail and some fresh provisions on board, and to have a look round the town. The streets seemed very quiet and dingy after Valetta, but the market is an extremely good one, and a walk through the galleries on the North Face is full of interest. The Alameda Gardens were looking very fresh and pretty. The busts of two of England's great men, the Duke of Wellington, and General Eliot, afterwards Lord Heathfield, who defended Gibraltar during the great siege from 1779 to 1783 are well placed in prominent positions. The lighthouse at Europa Point is also worth visiting ; a fine picture of the Rock can be obtained through the lenses of the lantern.

Weighed anchor for the last time before reaching England, and sailed at 5.30 P.M. getting a fair wind through the Straits.

Passed Cape St. Vincent about 11 P.M. on April 1st; from here to Cape Finisterre we experienced strong northerly winds which kept us back a good deal. On the afternoon of April 4th, when about four miles from Cape Finisterre, we once more fell in with the *Merlin* and communicated with her. Passed Cape Finisterre about 5 P.M., when it was still blowing fresh from the north-east.

By the morning of the 5th the wind had almost died away, and we had most favourable weather for our passage across the Bay—a bright clear sky, light northerly wind, and no sea, only a long swell, which gave the ship a fit of rolling every now and then.

On the evening of April 6th we sighted Ushant;
and about 4 A.M., on the 7th, saw the glare from the
Lizard lights, though we were at too great a distance
to see the lights themselves.

By daylight on the 7th we knew we could not be
very far from the Eddystone, but heavy rain and fog
shut out everything beyond a very short distance, and
we were within a mile and a half off the lighthouse
before it became visible. Passed the Eddystone about
8 A.M. The weather still continued very thick and
no land was visible for some time ; however, by nine
o'clock it began to clear, and at half-past nine, as we
made fast to a buoy in the Sound, the rain had completely cleared away, and all the well-known features
of the landscape were easily recognized.

Discharged invalids and supernumeraries, and sailed
at 5 P.M. for Portsmouth. Arrived at Spithead about
8 A.M. on April 9th. The day was fully occupied in
preparing for the inspection which took place on the
following morning. The Commander-in-Chief, Admiral
Sir John E. Commerell, G.C.B.,V.C., came on board about
10 A.M., immediately after the steam trial. Both the
trial and inspection were got through satisfactorily, and
at 5 P.M. the *Calliope* was lashed alongside the Pitch
House jetty, and the commission was virtually at an
end. The work of stripping the ship began next day ;
and April 30th was fixed on as the date for paying off.

It is satisfactory to note that the punishment returns
during the commission compare very favourably with
the general average of ships of the same class. Not
a single seaman or marine belonging to the ship was

tried by court martial. The only court martial case was that of a domestic. The number of men confined in gaol was unusually small; and the number of desertions considerably below the average for the Australian station. It is also noticeable that while the total number of punishments was small, the total for the last quarter was very much less than that for any previous quarter.

Throughout the commission the general health of the ship's company was extremely good. There was very little serious illness on board, and very few men were invalided. The number of serious accidents was very small. In only one case, that of William Rolfe, was an accident the cause of death.

EXTRACTS FROM ENGINE ROOM REGISTER.

Distance run during the Quarter ending	Under Steam Alone.	Under Steam and Sail.	Under Sail Alone.	Tons of Water Distilled.	Tons of Coal used for all Purposes.
31st March, 1887 . .	1566·1	804·8	1584·8	129	295·4
30th June, 1887 . .	1972·3	1230·9	7134·3	286	298·2
30th September, 1887	3819·5	2480·6	.74·7	368	761·6
31st December, 1887	4914·9	978·7	82·6	208	564·5
31st March, 1888 . .	2275·1	3118·7	217·7	262	702·0
30th June, 1888 . .	2268·8	2576·7	490·0	291	502·2
30th September, 1888	2645·1	1157·5	117·0	163	617·5
31st December, 1888	1215·2	2075·8	490·7	201	467.5
31st March, 1889 . .	2072·3	2890·2	69·9	335	631·9
30th June, 1889 . .	1706·6	1024·4	4·5	167	484·3
30th September, 1889	1733·2	1279·4	295·2	182	458·5
31st December, 1889	6776·2	4153·9	124·1	457	1232·0
31st March, 1890 . .	4652·2	3382·7	187.1	446	1257·0
30th April, 1890 . .	1030·0	140·0	—	33	207·0
Total	38647·5	27294·3	10872·6	3528	8479·6

Total distance covered during the commission 76,814 knots. From January 25th, 1887, to April 30th, 1890, the total number of days at sea was 528, and in harbour 663.

The *Calliope* is a 3rd class cruiser, of 2,770 tons; H.P. of engines, 4,020; length, 235 feet; beam, 44 feet 6 inches. Built at Portsmouth, and launched in 1884. Armed with 4 6-inch 5-ton B.L.R., 12 5-inch 38-cwt. B.L.R., 10 machine, 2 light guns, and 2 torpedo dischargers.

PORTS VISITED BY H.M.S. "CALLIOPE," 1887—1890.

1887.

Port.	Arrival.		Departure.	
	1887.		1887.	
Spithead	Jan.	27th	Jan.	30th.
Portland	Feb.	2nd	Feb.	5th.
Portsmouth	,,	7th	,,	25th.
Cowes Road	,,	25th	,,	26th.
Plymouth	,,	26th	March	5th.
Madeira	March	11th	,,	13th.
St. Vincent	,,	20th	,,	22nd.
Porto-Praya	,,	23rd	,,	24th.
Simon's Bay	May	5th	May	16th.
Anjer Point	June	27th	June	28th.
Singapore	July	2nd	July	3rd.
Hong Kong	,,	9th	,,	17th.
Nagasaki	,,	21st	,,	23rd.
Hako-date	,,	27th	Aug.	2nd.
Oterranai	Aug.	4th	,,	10th.
Vladivostock	,,	14th	,,	19th.
St. Vladimir Bay	,,	20th	,,	27th.
Goshkevitch Bay	,,	29th	,,	31st.
Port Lazaref	Sept.	3rd	Sept.	9th.
Gensan	,,	9th	,,	12th.
Fusan	,,	14th	,,	20th.
Hong-Kong	,,	26th	Oct.	7th.
Sydney, N.S.W.	Nov.	15th	Dec.	16th.
Russell	Dec.	24th	,,	30th.
Auckland	,,	31st	Jan.	5th, 1888.

1888.

Port.	Arrival. 1888.		Departure. 1888.	
Wellington	Jan.	9th	Jan.	16th.
Sydney	,,	24th	Feb.	4th.
Russell	Feb.	11th	,,	13th.
Auckland	,,	14th	,,	28th.
Port Lyttelton	March	3rd	March	8th.
Akaroa	,,	8th	,,	9th.
Port Chalmers	,,	10th	,,	14th.
Wellington	,,	17th	,,	22nd.
Sydney	April	2nd	April	14th.
Norfolk Island	,,	20th	,,	20th.
Suva, Fiji	,,	27th	May	1st.
Ngau	May	1st	,,	3rd.
Levuka	,,	3rd	,,	5th.
Apia, Samoa	,,	9th	,,	14th.
Ngau	,,	18th	,,	20th.
Suva	,,	20th	,,	28th.
Noumea	June	9th	June	13th.
Sydney	,,	19th	July	21st.
Melbourne	July	26th	Aug.	11th.
Sydney	Aug.	14th	Sept.	4th.
Lord Howe Island	Sept.	7th	,,	7th.
Norfolk Island	,,	11th	,,	12th.
Tonga-tabu	,,	17th	,,	25th.
Port Valdez-Vavau	,,	27th	,,	28th.
Pango-pango	,,	30th	Oct.	1st.
Apia	Oct.	2nd	,,	10th.
Somo-somo	,,	14th	,,	15th.
Suva	,,	17th	,,	19th.
Port Sandwich	,,	23rd	,,	24th.
Havannah Harbour	,,	25th	,,	25th.
Dillon Bay, Eromanga	,,	26th	,,	26th.
Noumea	,,	28th	,,	30th.
Sydney	Nov.	14th	Nov.	21st.
Jervis Bay	,,	22nd	,,	24th.
Sydney	,,	25th	Dec.	27th.

1889.

	Arrival. 1889.		Departure. 1889.	
Auckland	Jan.	4th	Jan.	12th.
Wellington	,,	15th	,,	21st.
Apia, Samoa	Feb.	4th	March	16th.
Apia	March	19th	,,	21st.
Sydney	April	4th	May	11th.
Adelaide	May	15th	,,	24th.

Port.	Arrival.		Departure.	
	1889.		1889.	
Melbourne	May	28th	June	2nd.
Jervis Bay	June	5th	,,	8th.
Sydney	,,	9th	July	9th.
Noumea	July	16th	,,	27th.
Port Inyung	,,	29th	,,	29th.
Dillon Bay	,,	31st	,,	31st.
Havannah Harbour	Aug.	1st	Aug.	1st.
Foreland Anchorage	,,	2nd	,,	2nd.
Port Sandwich	,,	2nd	,,	3rd.
Port Stanley	,,	3rd	,,	5th.
Tongoa	,,	6th	,,	6th.
Leper's Island	,,	7th	,,	7th.
Pentecost	,,	8th	,,	8th.
Ambrym	,,	9th	,,	9th.
Port Sandwich	,,	9th	,,	11th.
Havannah Harbour	,,	12th	,,	12th.
Noumea	,,	15th	Sept.	5th.
Sydney	Sept.	11th	Oct.	2nd.
Moreton Bay	Oct.	7th	,,	9th.
Cooktown	,,	14th	,,	16th.
Singapore	Nov.	6th	Nov.	9th.
Colombo	,,	20th	,,	24th.
Aden	Dec.	6th	Dec.	8th.
Suez	,,	16th	,,	17th.
Port Said	,,	19th	,,	20th.
Suez	,,	21st	,,	21st.
Aden	,,	29th	,,	31st.

1890.

Port.	Arrival.		Departure.	
	1890.		1890.	
Zanzibar	Jan.	7th	Jan.	11th.
Zanzibar	,,	17th	,,	29th.
Port Reitz	,,	31st	Feb.	7th.
Malindi	Feb.	8th	,,	8th.
Manda Bay	,,	9th	,,	10th.
Zanzibar	,,	11th	,,	15th.
Aden	,,	25th	,,	27th.
Suez	March	8th	March	9th.
Port Said	,,	11th	,,	12th.
Malta	,,	19th	,,	24th.
Gibraltar	,,	31st	,,	31st.
Plymouth	April	7th	April	7th.
Spithead	,,	8th	,,	9th.
Portsmouth	,,	9th		

APPENDIX.

OFFICIAL REPORT OF PROCEEDINGS.

H.M.S. "CALLIOPE," AT APIA, SAMOA,
20th March, 1889.

No. 19.

SIR,—Since the 5th instant, the date of my last letter of proceedings (No. 18), there has been nothing to remark on in the political state of affairs here, but I deeply regret to have to report a terrible hurricane, which has caused a disaster unprecedented since the introduction of steam ; the total loss of four men-of-war out of seven, with a loss of 130 lives, and the stranding of two others.

2. The *Calliope*, I thank God, is left afloat, and sound in hull ; though with loss of three anchors, three boats, and foreyard sprung, and all fastenings of bowsprit carried away. We lost no lives, and had only one serious accident, a carpenter's mate who has a fractured skull, but he is doing well.

3. The *Trenton*, which arrived on the 11th, the *Vandalia*, the *Adler*, and the *Eber*, are total wrecks ; and the *Olga* and the *Nipsic* are on a sandy beach, with but small chance of getting them off.

4. On the 7th and 8th we had a gale, to which we struck lower yards and topmasts and got up steam, but it did not do much damage, and all the men-of war rode it out without dragging.

5. On Thursday, 15th, the barometer began to fall, with heavy rain but no wind, and fell until 2 P.M. on the 15th, when it reached 29·11.

We, in common with all the other ships, struck lower yards and topmasts, and got up steam, so as to be ready for anything ; but we were assured by experienced people on shore that the fall was for rain, and that there was nothing to be afraid of. In addition to that we were lulled into comparative security by our having already had experience of three gales, and had ridden them out all right.

6. But as the afternoon of the 15th wore on, the wind came up from the N.E., and gradually freshened. By midnight it was blowing a gale, and it increased all through the middle and morning watch.

By daylight, when it was blowing a hurricane, we found we had dragged quite close to the reef. By that time the *Eber* had gone down with all hands but five.

7. The harbour was crowded with shipping, all dragging together. I got steam up in all boilers, and succeeded in keeping clear of the reef for some time, but soon found that that could not last for long. The

seas were perfectly fearful, breaking over our topgallant forecastle, and all but burying the poor *Adler*, which soon went on the reef. By very good management they slipped their cables at the right moment, and were lifted right on to the reef, where they lay on their broadside. Had they not slipped the cables, she would have gone down in deep water. Twenty men were drowned in her, the others found shelter in the ship till Sunday morning.

8. The seas were now (8 A.M. on 16th) breaking from out beyond the reefs. The *Vandalia* was dragging down on top of us, the *Olga* was close on our starboard quarter, and the shore reef close on the port quarter. I managed for some time to keep clear of all three, but our port cable parted and we came against the *Vandalia's* stern, and carried away the jibboom, and all the fastenings of the bowsprit. The spar itself was saved by lifting right up when the bobstay, bands, &c., went. Then the *Olga* came up on our starboard side and very nearly rammed us. I just managed to sheer clear, but she caught our foreyard and damaged it severely. Luckily it boomed her off.

9. Seeing that every time we tautened our cable we were getting nearer the reef (in fact it had become a question of feet), I made up my mind to slip and try to go out, reserving as a last resort the hope of beaching the ship on a sandy patch, which the *Olga* afterwards succeeding in reaching.

10. I called on the Staff Engineer for every pound of steam he could give us, and slipped the one remaining cable. I had slipped the sheet some time before, finding it did no good and hampered my movements. The engines worked admirably, and little by little we gathered way and went out, flooding the upper deck with green seas which came in over the bows, and which would have sunk many a ship. My fear was that she would not steer, and would go on the reef in the passage out, especially as the *Trenton* was right in the fairway. But we went under her stern, putting our foreyard over her quarter boat, and came up head to wind most beautifully. Once outside her, it was nothing but hard steaming ; if the engines held out we were safe, if anything went wrong with them we were done for. Thanks to the admirable order in which the engines and boilers have been kept, all went well.

We steamed from 9.30 A.M., when we slipped, until 8 P.M., with the extreme power of the engines, developing at least as much power as we have ever done on a trial, without a hitch, and that with the engines racing every plunge in a very heavy sea.

The wind increased during the afternoon still more. The best idea of its strength may be got from the fact that we made only a knot or so, against it and the sea, just enough to give steerage way. I did not dare to go slower, because the ship would have fallen off into the trough, and also, it being as thick as pea-soup, I could not tell if I was ten miles or ten yards off the reef which skirts the whole shore.

11. After 8 P.M., finding the sea going down somewhat, though it was blowing as hard as ever, I was able to reduce speed. By noon on the 17th it had blown itself out down to an ordinary gale. A passing glimpse of the sun showed us that we were well off the land.

12. I returned to Apia on the 19th (yesterday) and found the

harbour perfectly clear, not a craft, from the *Trenton* to a schooner, afloat in it. The *Vandalia* is under water to her nettings. She lost her captain and thirty men. The *Trenton* is under water to her main deck. The *Olga* and the *Nipsic* are above water all right but some feet in the sand.

13. The whole of the anchor-buoys have been washed away, and the anchors and cables of all ships have been mixed up by dragging one over the other to such an extent, that there can be no hopes of picking them up. In view of the possibility of another hurricane, the great probability of at least another gale, and our condition, with only one anchor and damaged spars, I have made up my mind that the safety of the ship requires that I should not stop an hour longer than necessary in Apia, indeed, that I should get out of hurricane latitudes as soon as possible. I have therefore ordered 150 tons of coal from the German firm who are alone able to supply us, and propose as soon as that is in (to-morrow probably), to leave for Sydney. I have so informed the Consul, who sees the necessity of that course, and who does not think that a man-of-war is now wanted, though he expresses his hopes of seeing one when the fine season comes round.

14. I cannot speak too highly of the conduct of every officer and man on board the ship. During the hours we passed, when any moment might have been our last, every order was obeyed with alacrity and without confusion, and the way in which the Engineer Officers and Stokers kept to their work is beyond all praise. It is a matter on which I feel very keenly, and I propose to submit a special report on the subject when I have more time. I am obliged to close this immediately for the mail.

15. We shall want, I presume, from England :—

3 anchors, 60 cwt., Admiralty iron stocked, fitted with band on shank, for stowing with one davit. 2 anchors fitted for starboard side and 1 for port.
14 lengths 2-inch chain (175 fms.)
3 anchor shackles.
11 joining shackles
1 8-cwt. kedge anchor.
3 ground chains.
3 slips for ground chains.
* Diving apparatus complete.

I have the honour to be,

Sir,

Your obedient servant,

(Signed)   H. C. KANE,

Captain.

To REAR-ADMIRAL HENRY FAIRFAX, C.B.,
   &c.,   &c.,   &c.,
Commander-in-Chief,
Australia.

P.S.—*At the urgent request of the American Admiral I have supplied him with our diving gear.

Letter from ADMIRAL KIMBERLY, U.S.N., to CAPTAIN KANE.
Consulate-General of the United States, America,
Apia, Samoa. (*Undated*).

MY DEAR CAPTAIN,—Your kind note received. You went out splendidly, and we all felt from our hearts for you, and our cheers came with sincerity and admiration for the able manner in which you handled your ship. It was a gallant thing, and you did it so well it could not have been done better. We could not have been gladder than if it had been one of our ships, for in a time like that I can say truly with our old Admiral Josiah Latnall, " That blood *is* thicker than water."

I thank you many times for your kind offer, but nothing can be done for us under the circumstances. We are trying to get a schooner off to-morrow to meet the steamer for Tutuila and Auckland, to send despatches for our Government and friends at home.

We have three anchors out in the harbour, and if they would be of any use to you, you are welcome to take them for your use if you can find the buoys. In regard to the boats we will let you have four, all we have left excepting our launch, so if you will man them they are at your service. I advise you to get away as soon as possible, as this harbour now is only a trap.

With congratulations for your happy escape.

Believe me,
Sincerely your friend,
(Signed) J. A. KIMBERLY,
Rear-Admiral, U.S.N.

THE END.

RICHARD CLAY AND SONS, LIMITED, LONDON AND BUNGAY.